BAHA'I FAITH
WORLD RELIGIONS

by
Paula Hartz

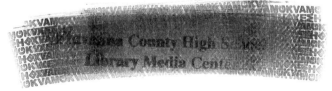
☑®Facts On File, Inc.

BAHA'I FAITH
World Religions
Copyright © 2002 by Paula Hartz

Facts On File, Inc.
132 West 31st Street
New York NY 10001

Library of Congress Cataloging-in-Publication Data
Hartz, Paula
Baha'i Faith / Paula Hartz.
        p. cm. — (World religions)
Includes bibliographical references and index.
        ISBN 0-8160-4729-4 (hardcover: alk. paper)
        1. Baha'i Faith. I. Title. II. Series.
BP365.H323 2002
297.9'3—dc21   2002003529

Facts On File books are available at special discounts when purchased in bulk quantities for businesses, associations, institutions, or sales promotions. Please call our Special Sales Department in New York at (212) 967-8800 or (800) 322-8755.

You can find Facts On File on the World Wide Web at http://www.factsonfile.com.

Developed by Brown Publishing Network, Inc. Series design by Trelawney Goodell. Design Production by Jennifer J. Angell/ Brown Publishing Network, Inc. Photo Research by Susan Van Etten.

Photo credits:
Cover: ©Eye ubiquitous/CORBIS; *Title page:* ©Vladimir Shilov; *Table of Contents page:* National Baha'i Archives, U.S.; *Pages 6–7:* National Baha'i Archives, U.S.; *11:* Courtesy, Baha'i International Community; *15:* ©Baha'i World News Service; *17:* Courtesy, Baha'i International Community; *20–21:* ©Baha'i World Centre; *24:* National Baha'i Archives, U.S.; *27:* ©Baha'i World Centre; *28:* ©Baha'i World Centre; *34–35:* Courtesy, Baha'i International Community; *37:* Courtesy, Baha'i International Community; *44:* National Baha'i Archives, U.S.; *46:* Courtesy, Baha'i International Community; *48–49:* ©Pat Humphrey; *53:* Courtesy, Bahai International Community; *54:* ©Baha'i World News Service; *59:* Courtesy, Baha'i International Community; *62–63:* National Baha'i Archives, U.S.; *69:* ©Baha'i World Centre; *72:* National Baha'i Archives, U.S.; *75:* © Vladimir Shilov; *78-79:* © Aima J. Marshall; *84:* © Pat Humphrey; *89:* © Pat Humphrey; *91:* National Baha'i Archives, U.S.; *92–93:* Courtesy, Baha'i International Community; *95:* Courtesy, Baha'i International Community; *99:* Courtesy, Baha'i International Community; *102:* Courtesy, Baha'i International Community; *104–105:* ©Vladimir Shilov; *107:* ©Vladimir Shilov; *108:* ©Baha'i World Centre; *111:* ©Bob Krist/CORBIS; *116:* ©Craig Lovell/CORBIS.

The author wishes to thank the National Spiritual Assembly of the Baha'is of the United States and its agencies for supplying information and assistance.

Printed in the United States of America

VB 10 9 8 7 6 5 4 3 2 1

This book is printed on acid-free paper.

TABLE OF CONTENTS

Preface

We live in what is sometimes described as a "secular age," meaning, in effect, that religion is not an especially important issue for most people. But there is much evidence to suggest that this is not true. In many societies, including the United States, religion and religious values shape the lives of millions of individuals and play a key role in politics and culture as well.

The World Religions series, of which this book is a part, is designed to appeal to both students and general readers. The books offer clear, accessible overviews of the major religious traditions and institutions of our time. Each volume in the series describes where a particular religion is practiced, its origins and history, its central beliefs and important rituals, and its contributions to world civilization. Carefully chosen photographs complement the text, and a glossary and bibliography are included to help readers gain a more complete understanding of the subject at hand.

Religious institutions and spirituality have always played a central role in world history. These books will help clarify what religion is all about and reveal both the similarities and differences in the great spiritual traditions practiced around the world today.

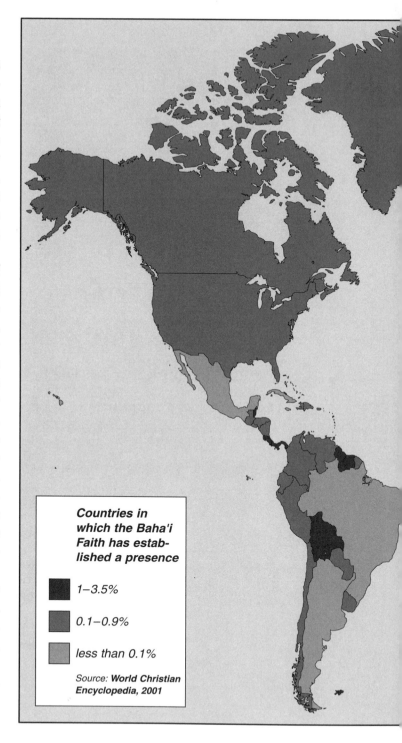

Countries in which the Baha'i Faith has established a presence

- 1–3.5%
- 0.1–0.9%
- less than 0.1%

Source: *World Christian Encyclopedia, 2001*

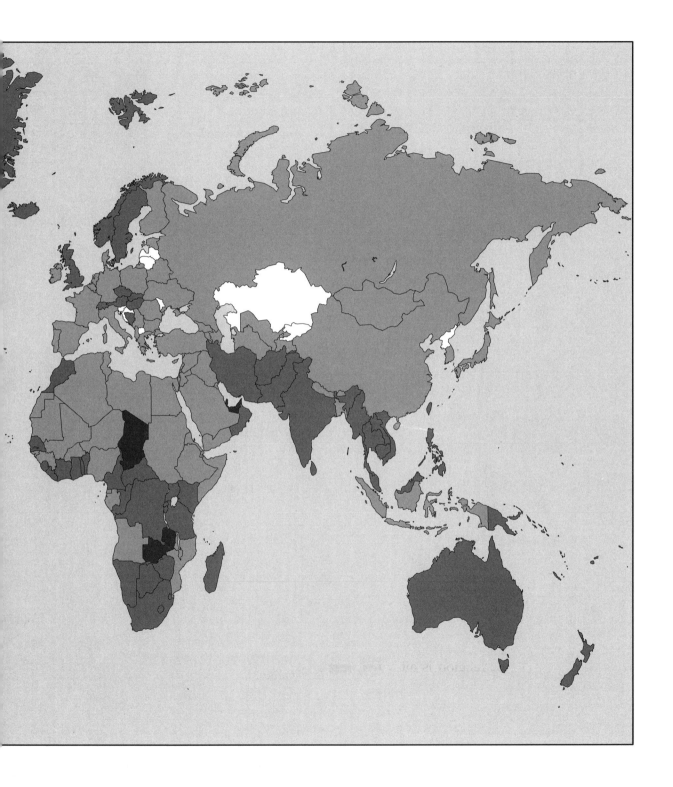

CHAPTER 1

Introduction:
The Baha'i Faith
and Its People

*T*he Baha'i Faith is the youngest of all independent world religions. It began as a small, local religious movement in Persia (now Iran) less than 200 years ago. Today the Baha'i Faith has nearly 6 million followers. It is one of the world's fastest growing religions. It is also probably the most diverse. It draws its membership from every religion, race, ethnic background, nationality, and creed in the world.

Distribution

Compared to world religions such as Christianity and Islam, each of which has more than a billion adherents worldwide, the Baha'i Faith is relatively small. However, Baha'is have established communities in 236 countries and territories around the world, making it the world's second most widespread religion after Christianity. It represents more than 2,100 ethnic, racial, and tribal groups. Baha'is live in more than 127,000 localities. There are organized Baha'i communities with elected local councils, called spiritual assemblies, in more than 11,700 places. There are national or regional elected bodies in more than 182 countries.

The Baha'i Faith spread to North America in the last years of the 19th century. In the past hundred years, it has spread to nearly every country and territory in the world. The largest Baha'i communities are in South Asia, Africa, and Latin America, as well as in some Pacific islands. The largest Baha'i community is in India. That country has more than 2 million followers, although that is still a small proportion of the total Indian population. In the United States, there are approximately 145,000 members of the Baha'i Faith.

■ Baha'is in the United States	
Number of localities where Baha'is reside	6,994
Number of local spiritual assemblies	1,171
Number of Baha'is in the U.S.	144,773
Baha'i schools and institutions	5

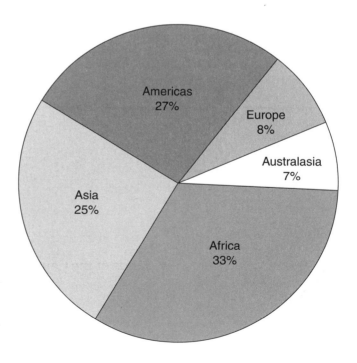

Americas 27%

Europe 8%

Australasia 7%

Asia 25%

Africa 33%

Central Figures of the Baha'i Faith

The Baha'i Faith traces its beginnings in Persia to a religious leader called the Bab (1819–1850). In 1844, the Bab announced that he had had a revelation from God. People began to follow him. A new religious movement began.

The Muslim religious leaders of Persia felt threatened by this new movement and its ability to attract followers. They persecuted the Bab and his followers. They had him arrested, beaten, and imprisoned. Finally he was executed by a firing squad for the crime of heresy.

The person who gave the Baha'i Faith its special character and shaped its spiritual and moral values is known as Baha'u'llah (1817–1892). He was one of the Bab's early followers. While he was in prison for participating in the Babi movement, he had a vision. He understood that God had called on him to be a divine messenger of God's word. He took the name Baha'u'llah, which means "Glory of God." After the Bab's death, Baha'u'llah rallied the Bab's followers. They gave themselves the name Baha'i—"followers of Baha."

Because Baha'u'llah was born a nobleman and had connections to the court of the shah, the Persian king, he escaped the Bab's fate. But he was banished from Persia and spent most of the rest of his life in exile and many years in prison.

When Baha'u'llah died in 1892, his will appointed his son 'Abdu'l-Baha (1844–1921) leader of the faith. He continued his father's work, strengthening and organizing the young religion. On 'Abdu'l-Baha's death in 1921, he left a will naming his grandson, Shoghi Effendi Rabbani (1897–1957), to succeed him as Guardian of the Faith. Shoghi Effendi created special plans that spread the faith to many different countries. He also translated and interpreted many of his grandfather's and great-grandfather's writings.

Shoghi Effendi died in 1957 without leaving an heir. The leadership of the faith passed to the Hands of the Cause of God, a group of Baha'i leaders Shoghi Effendi had named earlier to help him in his work. In 1963, Baha'is elected the Universal House of Justice, an institution that was originally planned and described by Baha'u'llah, to lead the faith in the future.

■ *A nine-pointed star is the symbol of the Baha'i Faith. The number nine is significant to Baha'is. Baha'u'llah received his revelation nine years after the Bab received his. As the highest single-digit number, nine symbolizes completeness. Baha'i temples are nine-sided, in recognition of that completeness.*

The Middle East today. The country of Persia occupied the area that became modern Iran in 1925.

Progressive Revelation

Baha'is believe in one God and Creator. But they understand that they cannot fully know God. God is infinite, and the human mind is finite. People know God because throughout history, God has sent divine messengers to the world to teach people God's will for them. These divine teachers are part of God's plan for humanity. They came to teach people about God and to move the human race toward greater spiritual, moral, and intellectual truth.

Among the divine messengers are Abraham and Moses of Judaism, Krishna of Hinduism, Zarathushtra of Zoroastrianism, Gautama Buddha of Buddhism, Jesus of Christianity, and the Prophet Muhammad of Islam. Baha'is believe that all of the leaders and founders of the great religions are equally messengers of the one God. They recognize the teachings of all these leaders as paths to salvation.

In addition, Baha'is believe that each of the divine messengers throughout history brought truth and understanding that was right for a particular place and time in the world. The moral and spiritual values they taught helped civilization to advance. The continuing advancement of humanity is part of God's great plan.

Today, we live in a much different world from that of leaders like the Buddha, Jesus, or the Prophet Muhammad. Although their teachings are still valid, we have reached a new understanding of the world. The world is coming of age. We can see that we all live on one planet, and that its future depends on global actions. Political, environmental, and social problems in one place are no longer isolated events; they affect the whole

■ Students at the New Era School in Panchgani, India, come from all over the world, reflecting Baha'u'llah's teachings that all humanity is one race.

■ *The Invocation symbol is another symbol that appears in Baha'i homes and buildings. It is the phrase **Ya Baha'u'l-Abha**, or "O Glory of the All-Glorious" in Arabic.*

■ *A Summary of Virtue*

Be generous in prosperity and thankful in adversity.

Be worthy of the trust of thy neighbor, and look upon him with a bright and friendly face.

Be a treasure to the poor,

   an admonisher to the rich,

   an answerer of the cry of the needy,

   a preserver of the sanctity of thy pledge.

Be fair in thy judgment, and guarded in thy speech.

Be unjust to no man, and show all meekness to all men.

Be as a lamp unto them that walk in darkness,

   a joy to the sorrowful,

   a sea for the thirsty,

   a haven for the distressed,

   an upholder and defender of the victim of oppression.

Let integrity and uprightness distinguish all thine acts.

Be a home for the stranger,

   a balm to the suffering,

   a tower of strength for the fugitive.

Be eyes to the blind, and a guiding light unto the feet of the erring.

Be an ornament to the countenance of truth,

   a crown to the brow of fidelity,

   a pillar to the temple of righteousness,

   a breath of life to the body of mankind,

   an ensign of the hosts of justice,

   a luminary above the horizon of virtue,

   a dew to the soil of the human heart,

   an ark on the ocean of knowledge,

   a sun in the heaven of bounty,

   a gem on the diadem of wisdom,

   a shining light in the firmament of thy generation,

   a fruit on the tree of humility.

—Baha'u'llah, ***Gleanings from the Writings of Baha'u'llah*** world. Baha'u'llah taught that this is the time for a single, unified faith with a global viewpoint. Baha'is see Baha'u'llah as the divine messenger for the modern age.

Baha'is do not worship Baha'u'llah, but they revere him as a great teacher. His writings are considered divine revelation. Baha'is also understand that in time, God will send yet more messengers to guide humanity. Baha'u'llah will not be the last. He promised that another messenger would come after him, after 1,000 years.

Baha'u'llah's message to the world is simple and straightforward: now is the time for worldwide unity. People must learn to get along with one another. They must begin to think globally. "The world is but one country, and mankind its citizens," he says.

Spiritual Beliefs

Baha'is believe that all people are spiritual in nature. Each person has a rational and everlasting soul. The soul is the real "self" of each individual. Each person's soul can be seen in his or her character; it shows in love and compassion, in faith and courage, in kindness and understanding.

According to Baha'i belief, the human soul needs spiritual nourishment in order to be fulfilled. The food of the soul is prayer, scripture, love of God, high moral values, and service to humanity. Time on earth should be devoted to developing the spiritual qualities that bring people nearer to God.

Baha'is believe that the soul lives on after death. When the human body dies, the soul is released into the world of the spirit, which has neither time nor place. The exact nature of life after death cannot be known, but Baha'u'llah says that death should be a time of great joy, when the soul returns to God.

A World Community

One thing that sets the Baha'i Faith apart from other world religions is its global perspective. Baha'is are perhaps the most diverse and widespread organization anywhere in the world. Baha'u'llah taught that as there is only one God, there is only one race—the human race. The time has come for uniting all people into one society under one faith.

A large number of Baha'is have converted from other faiths. They come from many different, and sometimes conflicting, backgrounds. Formerly, they may have been Christians or Jews, Buddhists, Muslims, Sikhs, Zoroastrians, or Hindus. Others come from African or Native American tribal religions. Some did not previously belong to any religion. Baha'is are not required to renounce their previous beliefs, but to accept a new unfolding of religious understanding. They understand that there is only one religion, and that is faith in God. All religions are therefore expressions of a single divine plan. For Baha'is, their faith fulfills the promises of all earlier beliefs.

Baha'is come from all races and ethnic groups and from different economic and social classes. Their faith absolutely forbids prejudice of any kind. They work together to break down barriers of prejudice and to build a global society in which all people live in peace and harmony.

■ *Pragyer for Serenity*

Oh God! Refresh and gladden my spirit. Purify my heart. Illumine my powers. I lay all my affairs in Thy hand. Thou art my Guide and Refuge. I will no longer be full of anxiety, nor will I let trouble harass me. I will not dwell on the unpleasant things of life.

O God! Thou art more friend to me than I am to myself. I dedicate myself to Thee, O Lord.

—'Abdu'l-Baha, **Baha'i Prayers**

The Baha'i Faith and the Individual

The Baha'i Faith places a great deal of responsibility on the individual. Unlike most other religions, it has no clergy. People are expected to read the scriptures for themselves and apply the lessons they find there to actions in their own lives. There are no sermons and no liturgy, or set order of worship. Instead, Baha'is meet on a regular basis to read scripture, discuss Baha'i issues and projects, and share fellowship. Depending on the size of the

■ *Baha'is read and meditate on scripture every day.*

The Greatest Name symbol is the word **Baha**, or "Glory," written in Arabic script. It appears on Baha'i temples and buildings. Baha'is may also wear jewelry engraved with this symbol.

community, they generally gather in Baha'i centers or in private homes. The Baha'i Faith does have houses of worship, but only seven of them in the entire world, and they are open to people of all faiths for meditation.

The Baha'i Faith emphasizes personal development. All people have both a spiritual and a physical nature. While people must satisfy basic physical needs for such things as shelter and food, they must recognize that the only way to be truly happy is to develop their spiritual side. This emphasis on spirit is what makes people truly human. Prayer and meditation open the soul to new possibilities. Being part of a diverse group breaks down prejudice. Baha'is abstain from alcohol and drugs, because these deaden the mind and the spirit.

Baha'i Unity

Although Baha'is celebrate their diversity, they understand that they must be firmly united in order to achieve their goals. The writings of Baha'u'llah and 'Abdu'l-Baha clearly establish the rules for holding the community together. There is one institution that is the final authority on any disagreements within the faith. That is the Universal House of Justice, at the World Center of the Baha'i Faith, in Haifa, Israel. This is an elected body that decides all Baha'i issues.

No individual is permitted to claim special understanding of the faith and start a sect. The Baha'i community is unified. As part of their covenant of faith, all Baha'is agree to accept the final authority established in the Baha'i scriptures.

Unlike the scriptures of Christianity and Judaism, which were written by many different people at different times, the scriptures of the Baha'i Faith were all written or dictated directly by Baha'u'llah and 'Abdu'l-Baha. And unlike the Koran, which contains passages that are difficult even for scholars to understand, the Baha'i scriptures are extremely clear and direct. Moreover, both Baha'u'llah and 'Abdu'l-Baha devoted many pages of writings explaining anything that their followers did not understand. So although Baha'is read the scriptures on their own and find their own meaning, they agree to abide by the authoritative interpretation of the head of the faith.

Baha'is and Social Policy

Baha'is learn that one of the most important ways of developing the spirit is through service to others. Helping other people is a characteristic of true humanity. Baha'is freely volunteer their time and talents to help others. Work also is a form of worship, because it profits both the community and the worker.

An important goal of the Baha'i Faith is that of promoting the well-being of humankind. Therefore Baha'is are engaged in a wide variety of social and developmental projects around the world. Wherever they go, they establish programs to teach and help their localities. These programs take many different forms, depending on the needs of the local communities. They may be tutorial schools, after-school projects, health clinics, classes in health care, agricultural projects, orphanages, environmental centers and tree-planting programs, vocational programs, women's centers, and many other programs to benefit society. Often a program starts in a Baha'i living room with a Baha'i volunteer and

■ *At the Baha'i Vocational Institute in Indore, India, young women learn sewing and other skills, as well as reading and writing.*

two or three students. All Baha'is understand that teaching and helping others is a fundamental part of practicing their religion, in the same way that attending worship might be for someone of another faith.

Baha'is finance these projects on their own. They volunteer their time and resources. Members also support the faith's social efforts with voluntary contributions. The Baha'i Faith does not accept contributions from outside its own membership. It is entirely self-supporting.

Baha'i Principles

Baha'u'llah left many writings that included the principles by which all humanity should live. His son, 'Abdu'l-Baha, who led the faith after his father's death, broadened them. The principles 'Abdu'l-Baha used to introduce the Baha'i Faith to people around the world remain the guidelines for living as a Baha'i:

- Each person must independently seek truth for him- or herself.
- All divine religions are one. Everyone worships the same God.
- Human progress does not occur through material things alone. Genuine progress comes from spirituality.
- Science and reason are in harmony with religion.
- The whole human race is one. All human beings are equally the children of God. People must wipe out all prejudices: religious, racial, political, national, and class.
- Extremes of wealth and poverty must be abolished.
- Women are the equals of men and are to have equality of rights, particularly of educational opportunity.
- All children must receive a basic education.
- There should be a single world federation with a single economy and a single language.

The Uniqueness of the Baha'i Faith

The Baha'i Faith is the only world religion to emerge during the modern age. Most other world religions are many hundreds, or even thousands, of years old. Judaism dates back more than 5,000 years, and Zoroastrianism more than 3,000 years. Native American and African belief systems are older than recorded time. Buddhism dates back about 2,500 years. Christianity began more than 2,000 years ago, and Islam more than 1,400 years ago. The earliest recorded works in Shinto are well over 1,000 years old. Even Sikhism, the next youngest world religion, is about 500 years old.

The Baha'i Faith's founders lived in modern times. 'Abdu'l-Baha, Baha'u'llah's son, lived to see such things as railroads, the telegraph and the telephone, automobiles, even airplanes. All the Baha'i founders were literate. They produced volumes of writing, most of which survives. Unlike religions such as Christianity and Judaism, whose scriptures were written perhaps hundreds or even thousands of years after the events they describe, Baha'i scripture is composed of the actual words of its founders, most often in their own handwriting.

There are more firsthand accounts of the Baha'i Faith's early years and its struggles, as well as of the people who brought it into existence, than of any other world religion. The Baha'i Faith thus presents a unique opportunity to see and understand how a new religion begins and how it grows and spreads.

CHAPTER 2

Foundations of the Baha'i Faith

*T*he Baha'i Faith grew out of religious influences in 19th-century Persia. Baha'u'llah, the founder of the Baha'i Faith, was born a Muslim. He revered the Prophet Muhammad, the founder of Islam, as a divine leader, and he followed Islamic customs and practices all his life. Therefore one important influence on the Baha'i Faith is Islam. Both Islamic scholars and Baha'is themselves have rejected the idea that the Baha'i Faith is a branch of Islam. The Baha'i Faith is a separate religion, distinct and different from Islam. However, the Baha'i Faith incorporates many Islamic ideals and practices, such as required daily prayer, giving to the poor, pilgrimage, and fasting.

Even more directly, the Baha'i Faith grew out of a religious movement that came immediately before it. This was the Babi faith, or Babism. Babis were followers of the Bab, a religious leader in Persia from 1844 until 1850. The Baha'i Faith's religious foundations rest on many of the teachings of the Bab, particularly his vision of a new social order and his promise that a new divine messenger was coming soon.

To understand the Baha'i Faith, it helps to know a little bit about the background from which it came: Islam and Babism.

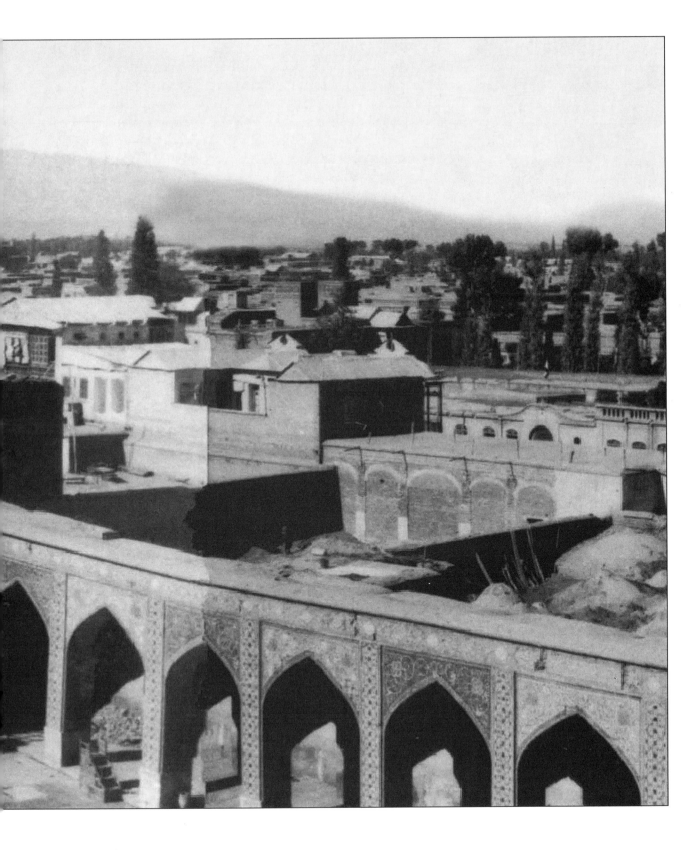

Islam Comes to Persia

Islam began in Arabia in the mid-seventh century C.E. About the same time, Arab armies conquered Persia, and by 652 a Muslim ruler sat on the Persian throne. Islam swept the Persian populace. By the ninth century, Persia was predominately Islamic.

Early in its history, Islam divided into two major sects. These were the Sunnis and the Shi'ah, which remain the two major branches of Islam today. In Persia, the birthplace of Baha'u'llah, the most important branch of Islam was the Shi'ah. Persian, or Iranian, Islam is known as "Twelver Shi'ah" because of the tradition of the Twelve Imams.

In the Shi'ah tradition, when the Prophet Muhammad died, he selected his son-in-law, Ali, to lead the faithful. Ali, in turn, passed the leadership down to his descendents. These chosen leaders were known as "imams." Early Persian converts to Islam believed strongly in the idea that the Prophet's chosen leaders provided a direct line back to the Prophet himself, and therefore to the will of God.

The Twelfth Imam

The line of Imams lasted through 12 generations. The 12th Imam was only a child when he became Imam. According to tradition, in the year 873 (the year 260 on the Islamic calendar) the 12th Imam withdrew from the world and was never seen again. People believed that he would come again to lead them into a new world of justice and harmony. Over time he became known as the "Hidden Imam," or the Mahdi, a title that meant "The One Who Would Arise."

The Shi'ahs believed that although he had disappeared from the world, for a time the last Imam still spoke to his followers. His words reached them through leaders they called *bab*, a word that means "gate." There were four *babs* until, in the year 941, the last *bab* died without naming a successor. Believers no longer had a direct link to the Hidden Imam, but they understood that one day a messenger would appear. This One would once again provide a direct line to the divine will of God for humanity. For the next thousand years, devout Persian Muslims waited for the return of the Hidden Imam.

The Bab Appears

In the mid-19th century, many people believed that the One promised in the Koran would soon come. In Persia, believers began to gather around a religious leader named Siyyid Ali Muhammad. *Siyyid* is a title of respect for descendents of the Prophet Muhammad. Siyyid Ali Muhammad was descended from the Prophet on both his mother's and his father's side. His relationship to the Prophet gave him credibility. To his followers, Siyyid Ali Muhammad was the promised messenger of God. They believed that through him they would receive truth and enlightenment. They began to call him The Bab. They called themselves Babis, or "followers of the Bab."

Siyyid Ali Muhammad was born on October 20, 1819, in Shiraz, Persia. Ali Muhammad was very young when his father died. He had little education, but he was exceptionally bright. Even as a child, he impressed adults with his understanding of scripture and of spiritual matters.

At 15, he became a merchant, like his father before him. By all accounts, he was a good businessman. He became known not only for his business ability but also for his honesty and fairness. After several years, when he was in his early twenties, he closed his business and traveled for a year to Iraq. He visited the holy cities of Islam and met Muslim leaders. On his return to Persia in 1842, he married the daughter of another merchant. The couple's only child died as an infant the following year.

Among those who knew him, Ali Muhammad became known for extreme piety and his great interest in religion. People began to remark on his holiness, and some even described him as a saint. Around this time, he began to have dreams in which holy figures of Islamic history appeared to him. He took these dreams as a sign that the spirit of God had come into his soul. He began to write down his thoughts on religious matters. As a rule, only trained religious scholars did such writing, and Ali Muhammad had no such training. But he felt divinely inspired.

The Bab's Declaration

On May 23, 1844, Siyyid Ali Muhammad announced that he was the bearer of divine truth. People attached great importance

The room in the Bab's house in Shiraz where he declared his mission on May 23, 1844.

to the fact that this was the year 1260 on the Islamic calendar— exactly 1,000 years after the disappearance of the Hidden Imam. At first, his followers understood him to be saying that he was the new gateway to the Hidden Imam, for whom they had been waiting. Later, they interpreted his words to be a claim that he was the Mahdi himself. Either way, he set in motion a religious upheaval that was to have lasting effects.

Beginnings of the Babi Movement

A man of great personal charm, the Bab had already begun gathering followers. One of these was a young religious student named Mulla Husayn. Mulla Husayn's studies had led him to believe that the Promised One of the scriptures would soon arrive. When he heard from Siyyid Ali Muhammad's own lips that he was the promised one awaited by all faiths, he immediately declared his faith. Within several weeks, 17 others had joined him. Another early follower was a young man named Muhammad Ali-i-Barfurush, whom the Bab called Quddus, or "Most Holy," and a young woman with whom the Bab was corresponding, later known as Tahirih, "The Pure One." The Bab called these first 18 followers the "Letters of the Living." He told them to go throughout Persia, spreading the good news that the Promised One was coming.

The Bab's Message

Many things about the Bab worked to convince his followers that he was a divine leader. He had a remarkable ability to explain passages from the Koran (the Islamic holy book). Scholars had puzzled over these passages for centuries. Highly spiritual, he had a strong effect on his listeners, who believed that his speech was divinely inspired. He revealed more than 100,000 new verses in the style and spirit of the Koran, which his followers believed to come directly from God.

Even more striking than his discussions of religious matters and spiritual revelations was his view for society. His vision was broad in scope. In his most important book, the Bayan, he wrote that a time was coming when new forms of learning and science would appear. He called on people to embrace learning and to help bring about a new society. He provided the principles for a Babi society. These included a system of laws for society to live by. They also laid down rules for matters such as marriage, divorce, and inheritance. Another section gives rules for the relationship between the Babi state and other nations. Above all, the Bab's vision was a peaceful one. He rejected the idea that converts could be won by the sword. He urged his followers to be gentle and cause no sorrow to others.

Babi disciples traveled to all the cities of Persia with the good news of the Bab's coming. It was news that people had been waiting for, and many accepted it eagerly.

Trouble for the Babis

Although the belief in the return of the Hidden Imam persisted among the Persian people, the clergy were less receptive to the idea. Indeed, the actions of the Bab's followers outraged them. In Islam, the Prophet Muhammad is the final prophet. His word, as recorded in the Koran, is perfect in understanding and revealing God's purpose. The Bab's followers were presenting his words as the newly revealed word of God. The Shi'ah clergy, therefore, saw the Bab's claim as heresy. Furthermore, it was a threat to their power. If people accepted the Bab as the true speaker for the Hidden Imam, he would become the highest authority in Islam, and they would have to take their orders from him. They immediately rose up against him.

The Shi'ah clergy held great power in 19th-century Persia. The country's ruler, the shah, supported the rulings of their religious courts. Their decrees, therefore, had the force of law, and the Persian army could enforce their decisions. They also used the power of the pulpit. When they preached that someone was a heretic, they could easily turn the minds of their congregations against him. It was a small step to rioting and civil unrest.

In spite of being labeled an infidel and a heretic, the Bab attracted followers across Persia. The Bab even began to attract some members of the clergy. This disturbed and angered Muslim leaders even more. Anyone who attracted followers was a threat to them. They had the Bab placed under house arrest in Shiraz. But even though the Bab's movements were restricted, his followers in distant cities were persuading more and more people of the truth of the Bab's claims. Also, people who came to visit him went away persuaded. The movement continued to grow.

One of the early converts was a man called Vahid, a religious scholar with a sharp theological mind. Vahid had connections to the court and may have been sent by the shah to find out more about this "Shirazi saint" who was attracting so much attention. The Bab converted Vahid as well. Winning members

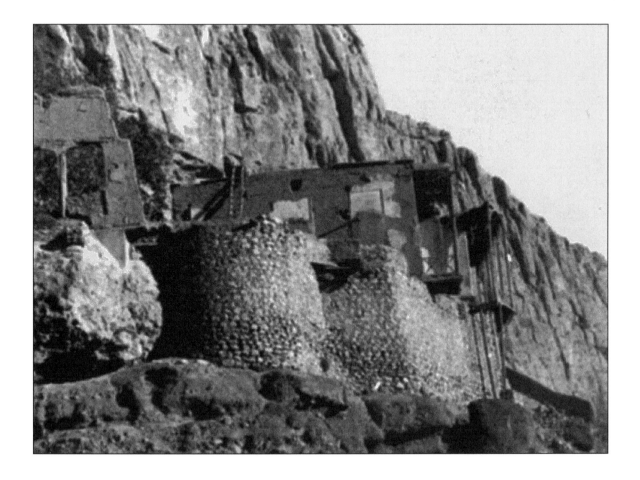

of the clergy to his side was an important step for the Bab in winning the minds and hearts of the people. More and more people were declaring themselves to be Babis.

Another of the converts who attracted attention was a woman known as Tahirih, "The Pure One." One of the most remarkable leaders of the Babi movement, she came from a family of scholars. In a time when few women learned to read or write, she studied the Koran with her brothers, and mastered its ideas easily. She was also a gifted poet. The young woman was much taken with the Bab's ideas and began corresponding with him. He quickly named her one of the Letters of the Living. She never met the Bab face-to-face, but their vigorous correspondence made her an important teacher of the emerging faith.

■ The fortress at Maku in Azerbaijan, where the Bab was first imprisoned.

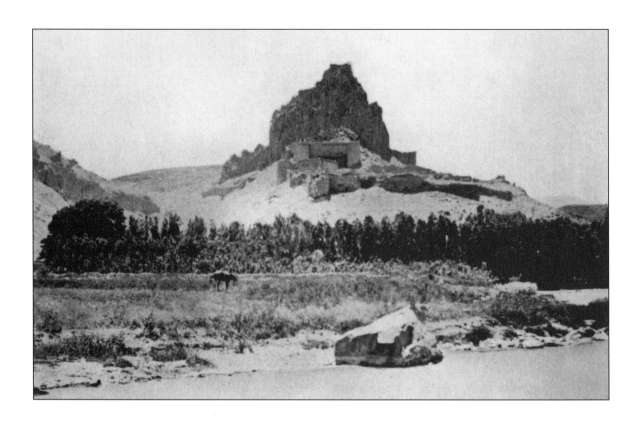

■ *The castle of Chihriq, near the Turkish and Iraqi border.*

Imprisonment and Trial

In September of 1846, the Bab was able to escape house arrest and leave Shiraz. He had hopes of traveling to Tehran to meet with the shah. Instead, the shah's prime minister had him arrested, taken to Azerbaijan, and imprisoned there. Azerbaijan, although part of Iran at the time, was far from the shah's court. The prime minister hoped that the Azerbaijanis would ignore the Bab's message. The opposite proved true. The new faith took root there. So the prime minister moved the Bab to a Kurdish area of Iran and threw him into the prison at Chihriq. This tactic, too, was a failure, as the Kurd leaders became admirers of the Bab.

Muslim clergy called for the Bab to be tried before a panel of religious scholars. In the summer of 1848, the trial took place. The Bab was sentenced to a cruel and painful form of physical punishment, the bastinado, in which the soles of his feet were beaten with sticks. During this torture, one of the men beating the Bab accidentally struck him in the face. The leaders called for a doctor. Dr. William Cormick, an Englishman, responded. He was deeply impressed with the Bab, whom he found to be mild and uncomplaining.

During this time, the traditional clergy continued to preach against the Bab. His followers came under increasing attacks from mobs that the clergy had aroused to violence. The mobs believed that they were waging a jihad, a Muslim holy war against unbelievers. The Bab's followers turned to him, hoping that he would bless their own fight against the people who were persecuting them.

The Bab, however, rejected the notion of jihad. Babis could defend themselves if their lives were threatened, but they were otherwise not to fight on behalf of the faith. The survival of the faith, the Bab decreed, was in the hands of God.

The Conference at Badasht

With the Bab in prison, leaders of the Babi faith met in the village of Badasht. One of their goals was to come up with a plan to free the Bab. Another was to share their understanding of the Bab's teachings, so they could go on leading in his absence. Among the leaders of the conference was the woman poet Tahirih. She electrified the conference when she announced that the Bab was not just a reformer; he was the Imam Mahdi, the Promised One. She went on to say that this meant that Babis were no longer bound by the requirements of Muslim law. As followers of the Bab, they must look to him for guidance.

She began by casting off her veil and head covering. Her action caused an immediate stir. Many of the more conservative Babis were shocked. They had never seen a woman unveiled in public. Even more, it caused the Muslim clerics to brand the Babis as atheists and their women as immodest and impure. But the Bab's doctrines clearly indicated that women were equal participants with men in the new religion.

Babis under Siege

The shah of Persia died in 1848, throwing the country into a state of political unrest. The Babis found themselves under

■ *The Bab*

[He] was a very mild and delicate-looking man, rather small in stature and very fair for a Persian, with a melodious soft voice, which struck me much....In fact his whole look and deportment went far to dispose one in his favor....

—*From the Memoirs of Dr. William Cormick*

even greater pressure from the Muslim clergy, who were trying to stamp them out. A group of Babis under Mulla Husayn had been traveling around the country proclaiming the Bab as the Promised One. They called on the people to follow him. The Shi'ah clergy preached vigorously from the pulpit that they were heretics. Rioting followed. The Babis withdrew to the shrine of a Muslim saint, Shaykh Tabarsi, and hoped it would be a safe place. They quickly put up a fort for protection.

But their troubles were not over. The clergy accused them of causing the riots. This time the government decided that the Babi movement must be wiped out. Officials sent a band of armed soldiers to add to the clergy and rioters already crying for Babi blood.

The Siege at Shaykh Tabarsi

Over the next year, more and more troops came and attacked the fort. They built a series of barricades around it, so the Babis were effectively trapped inside. Led by Mulla Husayn, the Babis had been able to beat back their attackers for a time. But eventually a few hundred Babis inside the fort were defending themselves against a large army, which was camped outside. The Babis were also running out of water. They managed to dig a well, but it was clear that their situation was becoming desperate. Mulla Husayn decided to charge the barricades. He knew he would probably die. He called on his companions "to partake of the cup of martyrdom" with him.

That day he bathed in the water from the well, dressed in clean clothes, and prepared himself for battle. Before dawn, he led his band of Babi fighters out of the fort. They broke through first one and then another set of barricades until they were finally outside. But their success was costly. A sniper who had climbed a tree shot Mulla Husayn in the chest. His companions carried him back to the fort, where he died a few hours later.

The End of the Siege

At last, the remaining Babis agreed to surrender. The army swore on the Koran that the Babis would be permitted to leave safely. But as soon as they left the fort, the army set on them again. Those who were not killed outright were tortured to death or sold into slavery.

This horrible scene played itself out in other towns as well. In Nayriz and Zanjan, the Shi'ah clergy aroused their followers to riot and then blamed the Babis. The government's troops joined in. People hunted the Babis down, seized their property, and killed them. Vahid, another respected Babi leader, died at Nayriz. At Zanjan, as at Shaykh Tabarsi, officials offered a pledge of peace signed on the Koran. As soon as the Babis came out, they were slaughtered. Some Babis were arrested and publicly executed when they refused to reject their new faith. A few, however, survived to tell what had happened.

The Death of the Bab

While all of this unrest was going on, the prime minister ordered the Bab's execution. The Bab had done nothing that was against civil law, however. So the prime minister had the Bab taken to Tabriz, where the clergy signed the death sentence for a crime against Islam.

Eyewitness accounts record the remarkable events surrounding the execution of the Bab. Their jailers suspended the Bab and one of his young followers by ropes from the top of a wall. A firing squad of 750 Armenian Christian soldiers lined up facing them. The order to fire was given. The rifles made a deafening roar, and black smoke filled the entire area. When the

> ■ **The Bab's Final Statement:**
>
> *Oh wayward generation! Had you believed in me every one of you would have followed the example of this youth, who stood in rank above most of you, and would have willingly sacrificed himself in my path. The day will come when you will have recognized me; that day I shall have ceased to be with you.*

> ■ *A Western Reaction to the Bab's Martyrdom*
>
> *This is one of the most magnificent examples of courage which mankind has ever been able to witness, and it is also an admirable proof of the love which our hero had for his fellow countrymen. He sacrificed himself for mankind; he gave for it his body and his soul, he suffered for it hardships, insults, indignities, torture and martyrdom. He sealed with his blood the pact of universal brotherhood, and like Jesus he gave his life in order to herald the reign of concord, justice, and love for one's fellow men.*
>
> *—A.L.M. Nicholas, a French consular official, 1850*

smoke cleared, the Bab's companion stood by the wall, unhurt. The Bab had disappeared.

Searchers found him in his room, calmly dictating to his secretary. The original firing squad was so shaken by what had happened that they refused to continue. Many believed that they had attempted to kill a holy man and now feared the wrath of God. Officials quickly brought together a squad of Muslim marksmen. This time the soldiers did not miss.

The story of the Bab's death spread throughout Persia like the wind. It had a profound impact not only on the Persian people but also on the many Europeans who lived in Persia at the time. It aroused new interest in his message—not just in his native country, but also in the outside world.

The Collapse of Babism

For the surviving Babis, however, the Bab's death was a disaster. In a few months, they had lost not only the Bab but also most of the Letters of the Living. Mulla Husayn had died in the siege at Shaykh Tabarsi, and Vahid at Nayriz. Quddus, the gentle young man and Letter of the Living whom the Bab called "Most Holy," was dragged through the streets in chains and finally tortured to death.

■ **The Death of Quddus**

...how, barefooted, bareheaded, and loaded with chains, he was paraded through the streets, followed and scorned by the entire population of the town; how he was execrated and spat upon by the howling mob; how he was assailed with the knives and axes of the scum of its female inhabitants; how his body was pierced and mutilated, and how eventually it was delivered to the flames!

Amidst his torments, Quddus was heard whispering forgiveness to his foes. "Forgive, O my God," he cried, "the trespasses of this people. Deal with them in Thy mercy, for they know not what we already have discovered and cherish."

*—from **The Dawn-Breakers***

In despair, two young Babis attempted to kill the shah. They did not harm him seriously, but the attempt aroused a new wave of violence against people who had done nothing but declare their faith in a man of peace and love. Babis were rounded up and tortured in unimaginable ways. Tahirih, the Pure One, although she had not been involved in the plot to kill the shah, was put to death. Defiant to the end, she is said to have looked her executioners in the eye and said, "You can kill me as soon as you like, but you cannot stop the emancipation of women."

The slaughter of several thousand of the Bab's followers, and his own martyrdom, left the Babis leaderless and disorganized. By 1852, it appeared that the new faith, begun in such hope, would vanish without a trace in complete failure.

The Bab's followers had found in him a messenger of God in the line of Moses, Jesus, and Muhammad, all founders and leaders of great religions. But his writings showed that the Bab did not see himself as the final prophet. The door was open for yet another leader—"He Whom God Will Make Manifest." The spiritual needs that had led people to follow the Bab remained strong. The seeds of a new religion had been planted, and in time they would grow again with renewed strength as the Baha'i Faith.

CHAPTER 3

Baha'u'llah, Founder of the Baha'i Faith

{O}ne important follower of the Bab escaped the fate of so many others. His name was Mirza Husayn Ali Nuri.

Mirza Husayn Ali Nuri was born on November 12, 1817, in Tehran, Persia (now Iran). His family were Persian nobles. His father was a landowner and a government official. The family was well-to-do and socially prominent, and the boy's father had a high position in the Persian court. Young Mirza Husayn Ali had no formal education; he was home-schooled. He read widely, however, and learned quickly. From an early age, he was devoutly religious.

Mirza Husayn Ali was 22 years old when his father died. Although he was young, officials offered him his father's government position; he turned it down. He preferred instead to stay at home, managing the family property and looking after the education of his younger family members. He also donated time and money to many charities in the region. In spite of his youth, he quickly came to be called "Father of the Poor" by the people in the region where he lived. He also gained a reputation for integrity and honesty at a time when many wealthy and important people were corrupt and dishonest.

Mirza Husayn Ali Converts to Babism

In 1844, Mirza Husayn Ali received a visit from Mulla Husayn, one of the Bab's early disciples. At the age of 27, Mirza Husayn Ali was already known for his good works and religious devotion. The Bab sent Mulla Husayn to Tehran to deliver a letter to Mirza Husayn Ali. As a result of receiving that letter, Mirza Husayn Ali became a follower of the Bab, along with four of his brothers and half brothers. His conversion was important to the Bab and to the Babi movement. Most early converts were religious students, like Mulla Husayn, or came from merchant or peasant classes. Mirza Husayn Ali's family were landowners with ties to the government. They were an important addition to the Babi cause.

From the time of his conversion onward, Mirza Husayn Ali Nuri worked energetically at spreading the Babi faith. He traveled across Persia to preach the Bab's message. Because of his wealth and high social standing, he had access to others in his social class, and he converted a significant number of people, including other members of his own family. He used his personal wealth to finance the teaching of Babism in other regions. His social position also helped to protect him from the persecution that Babi followers were beginning to experience.

Soon after Mirza Husayn Ali became a Babi, he began writing letters to the Bab, who was then imprisoned in Chihriq prison. The Bab responded with letters of his own, and Mirza Husayn Ali gained an impressive knowledge of the Bab's thinking. Other Babi leaders, such as Vahid, Quddus, Mulla Husayn, and Tahirih, drew him into their inner circle. They began to look upon him as an important interpreter of the Bab's teachings.

In 1848, Mirza Husayn Ali organized and helped to direct the gathering of Babis in the village of Badasht; this conference at Badasht gave Babism a new and more revolutionary direction. It was also at the Badasht Conference that Mirza Husayn Ali gave each of the Babis gathered there a new name, one that reflected their spiritual qualities. For himself, he chose the name Baha, which means "Splendor" or "Glory." After the conference, the Bab wrote to each of the participants, using the new name that Mirza Husyan Ali had given them. To the newly named

Baha, the Bab sent a rare and wonderful work of calligraphy, or handwriting, that he had done himself, in the shape of a star. It included the title Baha'u'llah, or "Glory of God," the name by which Mirza Husayn Ali Nuri came to be known.

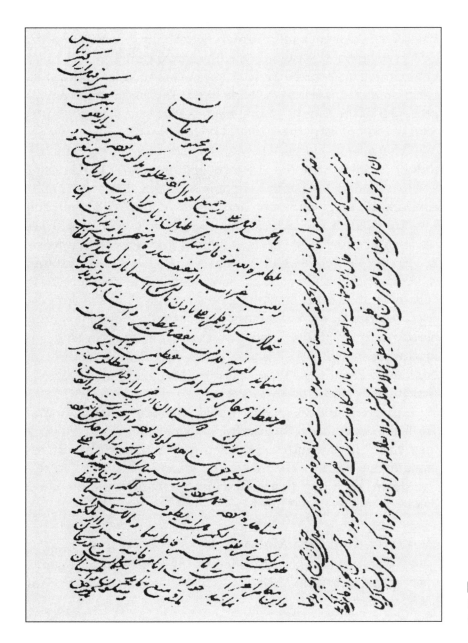

■ *Facsimile of a hand-written tablet, or letter, dictated by Baha'u'llah.*

Persecution Increases

The conference at Badasht drew attention to the Babis. The new movement was growing so fast that it was a threat to the existing order. Its members came under attack. It was at this time that officials arrested Tahirih and threw her into jail. Baha'u'llah tried to help her but was imprisoned himself and tortured by having the soles of his feet beaten with bamboo rods.

Free again, Baha'u'llah tried to convince his friends in the government that the Babis were peace-loving and would do no harm. In turn, his friends tried to persuade him to stop his work on behalf of the Bab, but he refused. He warned them that if the attacks did not stop, there would be trouble.

The attacks against the Babis continued, and trouble did indeed follow, with the attempt on the shah's life in 1852. Feelings against the Babis were now so strong that Baha'u'llah's connections to government and power could no longer help him. He was arrested and taken to Tehran, where he was locked up for four months in a prison so foul and terrible that it was known as the Siyah-Chal, or "Black Pit." Deep underground, cold, dark, and damp, it had once been a reservoir for one of Tehran's public baths. As Baha'u'llah described it, "The dungeon was wrapped in thick darkness, and our fellow prisoners numbered nearly a hundred and fifty souls: thieves, assassins, and highwaymen. . . . Most of these men had neither clothes nor bedding to lie on. God alone knoweth what befell us in that most foul-smelling and gloomy place!"

All over Persia, Babis were being persecuted and attacked. The Babi prisoners in the Siyah-Chal were chained together, so they could hardly move. The stench was so awful that they could barely breathe. They were under constant threat of torture and death. Each day, their jailers descended into the pit, chose one man, and executed him.

He Whom God Will Make Manifest

As Baha'u'llah lay in chains in the dungeon, he heard a voice speaking to him. The voice, which seemed to come from all sides, said:

Verily [truly] we shall render thee victorious by thyself and by thy pen. Grieve thou not for that which has befallen thee, neither be thou afraid, for thou art in safety. Ere long will God raise up the treasures of the earth—men who will aid thee through thyself and thy name, wherewith God hath revived the hearts of such as have recognized him. . . .

In spite of the filth and suffering that surrounded him, Baha'u'llah felt new power and strength. He understood that he was the person whom the Bab had promised, the one who was ordained by God to lead his people into a new understanding and faith.

Banishment

Somehow Baha'u'llah survived his imprisonment. Because of his family's influence, officials knew that they could not execute him without a trial. They also knew he had done no wrong, and there was no evidence against him. But officials were reluctant to let him go. They knew that he would immediately attract followers to the Bab's cause. Finally the prime minister, who was a relative of Baha'u'llah's, persuaded the court that Baha'u'llah should be banished from Persia. As part of his banishment, the government seized his property. They destroyed or seized all his books and works of art. They looted and burned his home. His possessions and property gone, still suffering from the beatings he had received and weak from his four months in prison, he was released without a trial.

Baha'u'llah came out of prison weaker in body but even stronger in spirit than when he was arrested. Under the conditions of his release from prison, Baha'u'llah had to leave Persia. He no longer had any possessions, but his family and followers could go with him if they wished. He chose to go to Baghdad, in what is now Iraq.

At first Baha'u'llah said nothing about the voice he had heard and its message. He settled in Baghdad and lived quietly with his family. Over the next three years, other Babis joined him and formed a small community.

BULGARIA
Black Sea
RUSSIA
Adrianople
Samsun
Sinope
Constantinople
Amasia
Gallipoli
Turat
Kilarfut
Mytilene
Sivas
Diyar-Bakir
OTTOMAN EMPIRE
Smyra
Mardin
Irbil
TURKEY
Mosel
CYPRUS
Kuikuk
Tehran
Mediterranean Sea
Akka
SYRIA
Baghdad
PERSIA (IRAN)
Jaffa
IRAQ
Port Said
Caspian Sea
EGYPT
ARABIA
Red Sea
Persian Gulf

■ Map showing the route of Baha'u'llah's exile.

Mirza Yahya

One member of the community was Baha'u'llah's half brother, Mirza Yahya, or Subh-i-Azal. Thirteen years younger, he had followed Baha'u'llah into the Babi Faith. After the conference at Badasht, the Bab had named Mirza Yahya as the one to be the head of the Babi Faith if the Bab were to die. At the time, the Bab was in prison, and he and Baha'u'llah both felt that Baha'u'llah could do the most good for the faith from behind the scenes. Since Baha'u'llah was both older and wiser than his brother, they believed that Mirza Yahya would continue to take his advice.

Unfortunately, Mirza Yahya was easily swayed. After the Bab's death, he fell under the influence of a Muslim cleric named Siyyid Muhammad. Siyyid Muhammad reminded Yahya that the Bab had chosen him, not Baha'u'llah. He persuaded Yahya to renounce his brother and proclaim himself the Babi authority.

Baha'u'llah realized that if he were to fight with his brother over the leadership of the community, the community would be weakened even further. He withdrew to the mountains, where he remained alone for two years. He later wrote of this time: "Alone, we communed with Our spirit, oblivious of the world and all that is therein." Baha'u'llah spent the time fruitfully by meditating and writing.

Baha'u'llah Returns

Meanwhile the Babi community in Baghdad was going through difficult times. Mirza Yahya proved to be a poor leader. Moreover, he could not answer theological questions as his brother had done. Would-be leaders fought for power, throwing the community into turmoil. Faithful Babis began searching for Baha'u'llah. Finally they found him in his mountain hideaway and persuaded him to return with them. By that time things were so bad that even Mirza Yahya joined in calling for Baha'u'llah's return. Baha'u'llah returned to Baghdad in March of 1856 and assumed control over the Babi community there.

During the next seven years, Babism experienced a rebirth. Baha'u'llah's reputation as a spiritual leader spread, and he attracted many new followers. He composed the Kitab-i-Iqan, or "Book of Certitude," which describes God's plan for humanity and explains Baha'u'llah's mission.

Baha'u'llah's growing reputation did not please everyone. Back in Persia, the shah once again felt that his power and authority were being threatened. He persuaded the government in Baghdad to move Baha'u'llah and his group farther away from the Persian border. This time they chose to move the group to Constantinople, which is now Istanbul, Turkey.

The Ridvan Declaration

Before moving to Constantinople, Baha'u'llah went to stay on an island in the Tigris River. In a garden there, which he called the Garden of Ridvan (Paradise), he gathered his closest followers around him and told them of the revelation he had received in prison. He was, he explained, "He Whom God Will Make Manifest," the divine messenger that the Bab and the

scriptures of other religions had promised. Today Baha'is celebrate the Ridvan Festival, as it is called, for 12 days every year,
from April 21 to May 2.

For the time being, however, Baha'u'llah's followers kept
his revelation a secret among themselves. The group arrived in
Constantinople in August, but they were not permitted to stay
long. Constantinople was the capital of the Ottoman Empire,
which was experiencing unrest. Playing on the fears of the
Ottoman rulers, the Persian shah represented the Babis as a
threat. He pressed to have them moved again. Wanting no more
trouble, the Turks agreed. So in December 1863, Baha'u'llah, his
family, and his companions were sent to Edirne, or Adrianople,
in European Turkey, still farther from Persian borders.

A New Religion Arises

If the shah had hoped to silence Baha'u'llah, he failed.
Visitors from all over Persia continued to flock to wherever
Baha'u'llah settled. The widely scattered Babi followers knew
that Baha'u'llah had drawn the Baghdad community back
together when it was on the verge of collapse. They turned to
him as their spiritual leader. Baha'u'llah decided that it was time
to announce his revelation to all the Babis.

Mirza Yahya was still the official head of the Babi faith.
Although he had wanted Baha'u'llah to come back to Baghdad
and help him out when things were bad, he had never fully
accepted his own loss of status. When the group moved to Edirne,
Mirza Yahya, still under the influence of Siyyid Muhammad,
began plotting to get his power back. When this failed, he twice
tried to have Baha'u'llah killed, but the attempts failed.

Baha'u'llah, in turn, sent Mirza Yahya an announcement in
which he pressed his claim to be He Whom God Will Make
Manifest and asked for Mirza Yahya's support. Instead, Mirza
Yahya claimed that he, rather than Baha'u'llah, was the one
whose coming the Bab had promised. Instead of the results
Mirza Yahya wanted, however, his announcement clarified the
differences between him and his brother and showed who was
the true leader. Almost all the Babis deserted Mirza Yahya and
accepted Baha'u'llah as the head of the faith.

The followers of Baha'u'llah now began to describe themselves as Baha'is, and the Baha'i Faith began to emerge as a separate religion.

The Proclamation of Baha'u'llah

The former followers of the Bab had accepted Baha'u'llah as their unquestioned leader. He now needed to establish himself and the new religion on the world stage. In 1867, he began writing letters to world political and religious leaders. In these letters, he proclaimed himself to be the One whose return had been promised in the Torah, the New Testament, and the Koran.

Baha'u'llah told of the coming of a new world order. Its outcome would be a world civilization that recognized the oneness of the human race. "The earth," he wrote, "is but one country, and mankind its citizens." He explained that governments were meant to serve the causes of international peace, social justice, and world unity. Governments that did not work for these goals would bring disaster on themselves.

In many parts of the world, Baha'u'llah's letters had little effect. But in Iran, where the shah felt insecure in his seat of power, they set off a strong reaction. Mirza Yahya, still smarting from his loss of prestige and power in the Babi community, saw the letters as a way to play on the shah's fears. He and others, such as Siyyid Muhammad, wrote letters accusing Baha'u'llah of trying to overthrow the Ottoman government in Constantinople, which was already weak from years of fighting. The Persian ambassador to Constantinople pointed to the letters as proof. He pointed to the steady stream of visitors that Baha'u'llah attracted and hinted that these people were up to no good. Finally the ruler in Constantinople ordered that the group in Adrianople be imprisoned in the fortress at what is now Akka, Israel (formerly Acre, Palestine).

On August 21, 1868, soldiers rounded up Baha'u'llah and his family and followers, about 80 in all, and put them on a boat to Akka. After a miserable 10 days on a stormy Mediterranean Sea, they reached land and were taken to prison under heavy guard. Ironically, one of those deported to Akka along with Baha'u'llah was Siyyid Muhammad, who had plotted against him.

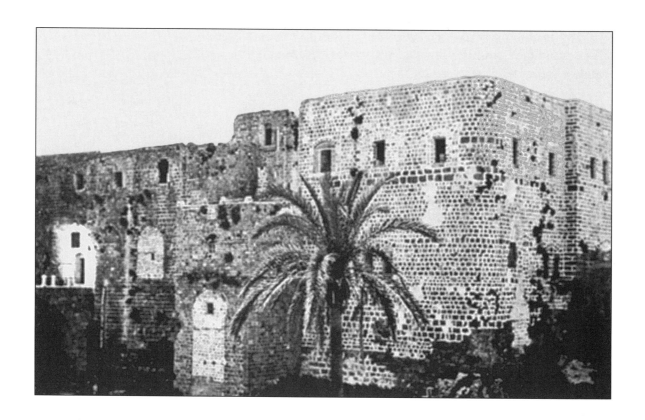

Imprisonment at Akka

The penal colony at Akka was a grim and terrible place. It was a prison city where the worst criminals from all over the Ottoman Empire were sent. It lay on the shores of the Mediterranean Sea and so was constantly awash in its tides. Its buildings were damp and crumbling; rotting refuse washed into it. The officials who sent Baha'u'llah there frankly hoped he would not survive. A number of the group did die, including Baha'u'llah's second son.

A small group of Babis remained loyal to Yahya and called themselves Azalis. They continued to harass the Baha'is, and they tried to convince the Ottoman authorities that the Baha'is were plotting against them. A group of angry Baha'is finally rose up and killed their tormentors, an event that caused Baha'u'llah great distress. He rejected all violence, no matter what the circumstances. Its use by his followers brought him deep grief.

In spite of the dreadful conditions, Baha'u'llah continued to preach goodness and to live according to his beliefs. He lived in the Akka prison for nine years, first inside the prison walls and then under house arrest within the city of Akka. Nevertheless, he managed to establish contact with the Baha'is in Iran. And it was at this time that he also wrote one of the great works of Baha'i scripture, the Kitab-i-Aqdas, or Most Holy Book. Gradually, his profound goodness and faith began to win over his jailers, and the prisoners' situation improved.

The Last Years of Baha'u'llah

By 1877, prison officials were no longer bothering to enforce the orders that had kept the Baha'is behind bars. Baha'u'llah was free to come and go. He moved to a mansion his followers bought for him at Bahji, outside the city. There he lived quietly, writing, meditating, and enjoying his gardens. He also received visitors from the many places to which the Baha'i Faith had begun to spread. One visitor was an English scholar, Edward Granville Browne, whom Baha'u'llah impressed deeply. "No need to ask in whose presence I stood," wrote Browne, ". . . I bowed myself before the one who is the object of a devotion and love which kings might envy and emperors sigh for in vain."

> ■ . . . *Those piercing eyes seemed to read one's very soul; power and authority sat on that ample brow; while the deep lines on the forehead and face implied an age which the jet-black hair and beard flowing down in indistinguishable luxuriance almost to the waist seemed to belie . . .*
> —Edward Granville Browne

Baha'u'llah lived until 1892. He died at the age of 74. For more than 40 years of his life, he had been a prisoner and an exile from his home. Born to luxury and wealth, he experienced poverty, hunger, grief, injustice, and suffering firsthand. He had

A view of the mansion at Bahji, showing the gardens. To the right is the small shrine where Baha'u'llah is buried.

been chained and beaten. He had even watched his children die in the brutal conditions of imprisonment. The religion that began with him reflects his deep identification with the poor and the suffering of the world.

During Baha'u'llah's last years, the young Baha'i Faith continued to spread. It now reached into Egypt, Russia, Turkey, Central Asia, and even India. It continued to grow in Persia, its birthplace. In spite of everything that governments and a powerful clergy could throw at it—persecution, angry mobs, and official injustice—it would not be stamped out.

In his will, Baha'ullah named his oldest surviving son, 'Abdu'l-Baha, to be leader of the faith after him. He also left instructions for taking the developing religion into the 20th century, which was fast approaching.

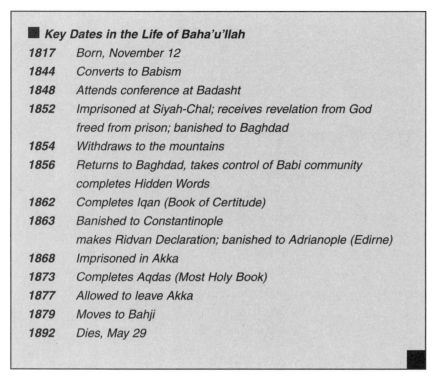

■ **Key Dates in the Life of Baha'u'llah**

1817	*Born, November 12*
1844	*Converts to Babism*
1848	*Attends conference at Badasht*
1852	*Imprisoned at Siyah-Chal; receives revelation from God*
	freed from prison; banished to Baghdad
1854	*Withdraws to the mountains*
1856	*Returns to Baghdad, takes control of Babi community*
	completes Hidden Words
1862	*Completes Iqan (Book of Certitude)*
1863	*Banished to Constantinople*
	makes Ridvan Declaration; banished to Adrianople (Edirne)
1868	*Imprisoned in Akka*
1873	*Completes Aqdas (Most Holy Book)*
1877	*Allowed to leave Akka*
1879	*Moves to Bahji*
1892	*Dies, May 29*

CHAPTER 4

The Baha'i Scriptures

*T*he Baha'i scriptures include the writings of the faith's three central figures. They are Baha'u'llah, his son 'Abdu'l-Baha, and the Bab.

The Writings of Baha'u'llah

For Baha'i believers, the writings of Baha'u'llah are the divine word of God. Baha'u'llah's books include Kalimat-i-Maknunih (which means "The Hidden Words," written around 1858); Kitab-i-Iqan, ("The Book of Certitude," 1862); and Kitab-i-Aqdas ("Most Holy Book," 1873). He also wrote many "tablets" or letters. He himself estimated that a collection of his letters would make over a hundred volumes. All of these works and others convey Baha'u'llah's message and lay down rules for leading the Baha'i life.

One important source of scripture for the Baha'i Faith is *Gleanings from the Writings of Baha'u'llah*. This is a collection of Baha'ullah's writings. It was compiled and translated into English by his great-grandson, Shoghi Effendi. From the more than 15,000 tablets Baha'u'llah produced in his lifetime, Shoghi Effendi chose passages that he felt would show the spirit of Baha'i teachings.

The Translations

Shoghi Effendi was Baha'u'llah's principal translator. He spoke fluent English as well as Persian and Arabic. After 'Abdu'l-Baha's death, Shoghi Effendi became Guardian of the Faith, as his grandfather's will stated. As Guardian, he was the only person with the authority to interpret Baha'u'llah's message.

It was Shoghi Effendi who set the style for the Baha'i scriptures. He chose a formal and older style, similar to the style of the King James Version of the Christian Bible. Shoghi Effendi believed that this style more closely reflected the stately Persian and Arabic that Baha'u'llah used. Shoghi Effendi also chose to use the word *mankind* to refer to all humanity and the masculine pronouns *he* and *him* to refer to God. He may have done so because the masculine form was considered the proper formal usage in written English when he was writing. Baha'u'llah's teachings do not attach any gender to the creator. Baha'i readers understand that words like *men* and *mankind* refer to all humanity, not just men.

Shoghi Effendi's translations into English are the highest authority for interpreting Baha'u'llah's writings. Translators use them, not the original Persian or Arabic works, when they translate Baha'u'llah's writings into other languages.

The Teachings of Baha'u'llah

Baha'u'llah's message reaches to the whole world. His vision is of a global religion that embraces all peoples of the earth. All people, whatever their country of origin, their race, or their ethnic background, are basically the same. Baha'u'llah recognizes only one race—the human race. He asks his followers to act in the best interests of all humankind.

The Hidden Words

In the Kalimat-i-Maknunih, or Hidden Words, Baha'u'llah restates the essential spiritual truths and ethical teachings that founders of all world religions have taught. The Hidden Words is quite short. It has only 52 pages. There are two sections: Words from the Arabic, with 71 numbered passages, and Words from the Persian, with 82. Each passage is only a few lines long. As in the scriptures of other faiths, the passages take the form of the voice of God speaking to the reader.

In the Arabic Hidden Words, God advises his children. "My first counsel is this: Possess a pure, kindly and radiant heart."His words urge believers to love him and only him. The Words also remind human beings of the great love God has for them.

The Persian Hidden Words carry a similar message. In this section, Baha'u'llah often uses metaphors of nature. He compares the word of God to seeds of divine wisdom and asks believers to let these words grow in their hearts. In this way, beautiful flowers of knowledge and wisdom will grow in the hearts of humankind.

The Book of Certitude

The Kitab-i-Iqan, or Book of Certitude, presents one of the great themes of Baha'u'llah's teachings. This is the theme of the progressive nature of religion. Many Baha'i scriptures enlarge on this teaching. The Book also deals with great religious questions, such as the nature of God, the nature of humanity, and the purpose of life.

According to the message of the Iqan, there is one eternal God, the Creator. The essence of God is unknowable. However, throughout time, God has revealed God's will and purpose for humanity through a chosen individual, or messenger. Each messenger has founded a great religion. For example, through Abraham, the Jews came to understand the oneness of God. Moses revealed God's law in the Ten Commandments. Jesus taught the love of God and the love of humankind. Each messenger has perfectly reflected the energy and power of God that is God's love.

> ■ *My first counsel is this: Possess a pure, kindly and radiant heart, that thine may be a sovereignty ancient, imperishable, and everlasting.*
> —*The Hidden Words of Baha'u'llah, Part I*, 1

According to Baha'u'llah, every divine messenger has come at a time that was right for a particular point in history. Although they have appeared in different times and places, they had a shared purpose. Each of these chosen leaders was right for his time and place and led people to a new understanding of God's will for humanity.

Many people have believed that the messenger of God will return, yet each messenger of God has been rejected in his time.

All have undergone hardship and suffering. Baha'u'llah points out that many prophets of God have had to suffer because of what they preached. Jesus suffered and died on the cross. The Prophet Muhammad of Islam cried, "No Prophet of God hath suffered such harm as I have suffered." To the messengers such as Moses, Jesus, and Muhammad, Baha'u'llah adds the Bab, who died for his teachings. Such persecutions have led people of their own time to doubt that the messengers were from God. Yet history proved that they indeed were.

In the Iqan, Baha'u'llah writes that 1,280 years have passed since the last messenger, the Prophet Muhammad. The time for a new messenger has come. He sees in people a yearning for the truth and the need for a new leader.

The spiritual aspects of the human relationship to God do not change. However, the conditions of life change from age to age. As time moves on, God sends new messengers with messages that are appropriate to each new age. In this way, religion evolves, moving forward with time.

The Most Holy Book

The Kitab-i-Aqdas is Baha'u'llah's book of holy law. He produced it during his prison years in Akka, probably the darkest and most difficult time of his life. For Baha'is, it is his most

---

■ *How the Words of Baha'u'llah Were Recorded*

From a contemporary account:

"Mirza Aqa Jan [Baha'u'llah's secretary] had a large ink-pot the size of a small bowl. He also had available about ten to twelve pens and large sheets of paper in stacks . . . He would bring [letters] into the presence of Baha'u'llah and, having obtained permission, would read them. Afterwards [Baha'u'llah] would direct him to take up his pen. . . .

Such was the speed with which he used to write the revealed Word that the ink of the first word was scarcely yet dry when the whole page was finished. It seemed as if someone had dipped a lock of hair in the ink and applied it over the whole page. . . ." Then the letters were transcribed and approved by Baha'u'llah.

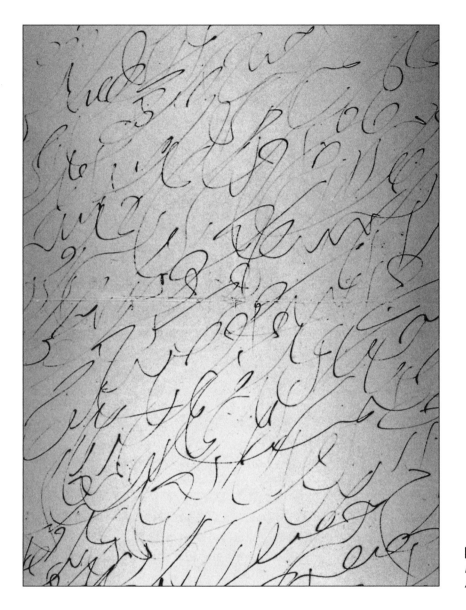

■ *An example of the notes dictated to Mirza Aqa Jan by Baha'u'llah.*

important work. The Aqdas lays out the rules for building a new world order in which all humanity will come together under the law of God. It names and describes the institutions that will make the new world order possible. It is the guidebook for the future world society that Baha'u'llah came to establish. The main part of the Aqdas is only 190 paragraphs long, yet it covers many topics.

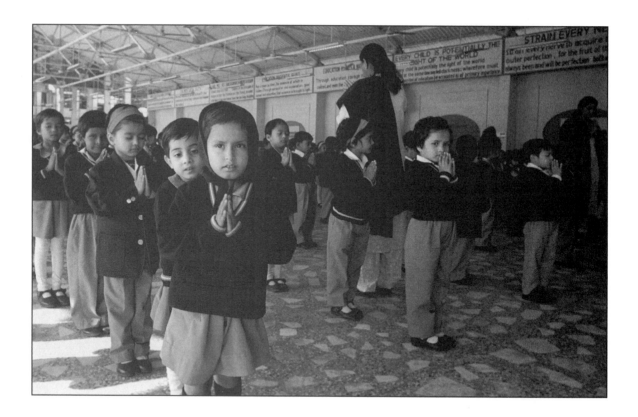

City Montessori School in Lucknow, India, teaches the essential principles of all religions to children from pre-school to college. The school stresses academic excellence, globalism, and interfaith harmony.

Religious Obligations

The Aqdas commands humanity to recognize Baha'u'llah as the messenger of God for this time and to obey the laws that God has given. The laws are designed to further the cause of bringing together the whole world under the Baha'i Faith.

From earlier religions, Baha'u'llah retains practices such as fasting and prayer that serve a spiritual purpose. He provides specific rules for prayer, including washing the hands and face before praying, the times when prayers are to be said, and which prayers are obligatory. He forbids congregational prayer, except for the dead.

Baha'u'llah establishes the Baha'i calendar and its holy days, and makes fasting obligatory during the 19-day month before the New Year. However, he creates exemptions from the fast for people who are ill, children, old people, pregnant and nursing women, and those doing heavy labor.

Social Laws

Social laws cover marriage, divorce, and inheritance. The Aqdas establishes the Huququ'llah, the voluntary wealth tax that all Baha'is pay to the faith. Baha'u'llah calls this tax "the Right of God." It supports the work of the faith.

Like the Ten Commandments of the Jewish Torah, the Aqdas forbids killing, stealing, lying, and adultery. In addition, it prohibits arson, gambling, alcoholic beverages, drug abuse, and gossip. Particularly, his followers are not to indulge in backbiting—talking about people behind their backs. Other prohibited activities are laziness, striking or wounding anyone, and creating conflict. Baha'is are to repent of their sins, but the mostly Christian practice of confession to another is prohibited. Baha'u'llah says, "[L]et repentance be between yourselves and God."

Rules for Living the Baha'i Life

The Aqdas exhorts believers to welcome followers of all religions in fellowship. They are to honor their parents, to study and to teach the faith, and not to wish for others what they would not wish for themselves. Parents are to educate their children in reading and writing, and especially in the rules of the Baha'i Faith.

Each individual is to have a trade or a craft. People are to use their skills in a way that will profit both themselves and others. They are not to be lazy or idle. Work is considered a form of worship. Baha'is are to care for their health and to be personally clean. They are to bathe regularly and to wear only clean clothes.

The Institutions of the Baha'i Faith

In the Aqdas, Baha'u'llah also sets down practical rules for the internal structure of the Baha'i Faith. He describes the establishment of Houses of Justice in each city and a world-wide Universal House of Justice that would rule on matters of faith not specifically addressed in Baha'i scriptures. He describes the institution of Guardianship to lead the faith after him. The Aqdas thus anticipated many of the institutions that the young religion would need as it grew and spread under new leadership.

The Message of the Aqdas

The Aqdas is the guide for the new world order that Baha'u'llah has come to establish: if humanity will follow its commandments, the world will be united as one country; war, famine, and suffering will end; and peace will rule the earth. The laws of the Aqdas are not Baha'u'llah's but God's. Baha'u'llah calls these laws "the Counsel of God"; they are God's word, God's bounty, and God's treasure, for those who will listen and take them to heart. Baha'u'llah writes that the Aqdas is the beginning of divine knowledge, the lamp that will lead all the people of the world humanity in the path of truth.

Supplementary Texts

The Aqdas also includes supplementary materials that Baha'u'llah revealed after the Aqdas was completed. The first of these is the Tablet of Ishraqat, which instructs Baha'is to obey the rulings of the House of Justice and to act according to the rules in the Aqdas. All are to come together, as God wishes, for, "Ye are all the leaves of one tree and the drops of one ocean."

Also included are the texts of the Obligatory Prayers. These are the Long Obligatory Prayer, the Medium Obligatory Prayer, the Short Obligatory Prayer, and the Prayer for the Dead.

Finally, there is a section of Questions and Answers. Here, Baha'u'llah clarifies fine points of the laws in the Aqdas, so there can be no misunderstandings or arguments about interpreting their message.

■ *The purpose of the one true God in manifesting Himself is to summon all mankind to truthfulness and sincerity, to piety and trustworthiness, to resignation and submissiveness to the will of God, to forbearance and kindliness, to uprightness and wisdom. His object is to array every man with the mantle of a saintly character, and to adorn him with the ornament of holy and goodly deeds.*

—Baha'u'llah, **Gleanings from the Writings of Baha'u'llah**

The Seven Valleys

The Seven Valleys is an essay that traces the journey of the soul toward the Divine Being. The Seven Valleys reveals Baha'u'llah's mystical side. He wrote it following his two years alone in the mountains. In this book Baha'u'llah quotes from the Koran, and also from the Sufis, Persian poets of the 13th century. Sufis were Islamic mystics who believed that they could reach the presence of God directly through meditation and prayer.

In his essay, Baha'u'llah traces the journey of the soul through seven valleys. These are the Valleys of Search, Love, Knowledge, Unity, Contentment, Wonderment, and finally to the Valley of True Poverty and Absolute Nothingness. This is the Valley of "dying from self and living in God, of the being poor in self and rich in the Desired One." This is the goal and the end of the spiritual journey. At last, the seeker will see the Beloved. Having taken the right path, the seeker finds peace.

The Works of 'Abdu'l-Baha

In addition to the works of Baha'u'llah, his son 'Abdu'l-Baha's writings are also part of the Baha'i scriptures. More than 27,000 of 'Abdu'l-Baha's letters survive. Many of 'Abdu'l-Baha's works explain and enlarge on Baha'u'llah's writings and echo his themes. "Man is, in reality, a spiritual being, and only when he lives in the spirit is he truly happy," he writes. But many of his writings reveal focus on the Baha'i social message.

Words into Action

One of 'Abdu'l-Baha's themes is that good ideas must be carried into action. People all over the world admire beautiful sayings and noble thoughts, 'Abdu'l-Baha says, but few of these ideas get carried into action. He goes on to say:

But Baha'is must not be thus; they must rise above this condition. Actions must be more to them than words. By their actions they must be merciful and not merely by their words.

Let your actions cry aloud to the world that you are indeed Baha'is, for it is actions that speak to the world and are the cause of the progress of humanity.

Racial Equality

Another of 'Abdu'l-Baha's themes is racial equality. He sees racial prejudice as an illusion and a superstition. It is the cause of much discord and war. He calls on Baha'is to reject all racial and ethnic prejudice absolutely:

All men are servants of the One God. One God reigns over all the nations of the world and has pleasure in all His children. All men are of one family; the crown of humanity rests on the head of every human being.

The Baha'i Faith teaches that all of God's children are equal in God's sight. God does not favor one nation over another. Therefore, divisions that separate nations, races, and ethnic groups are artificial barriers. They are nothing but superstition and tradition. They bring discord and hatred among people who must learn that they are one.

Rather than racial and ethnic division, Baha'is should be aware of the beauty of diversity. They should think of humankind as being like a beautiful garden, full of flowers, trees, and shrubs. Each flower has its own beauty, perfume, and color. Each tree is different as well, with different leaves, flowers, and fruits. But they all come from the same earth. They all share the same sun and rain. According to 'Abdu'l-Baha:

*So it is with humanity. It is made up of many races, and
its peoples are of different color—white, black, yellow,
brown and red—but they all come from the same God,
and all are servants to Him. . . . Let us look . . . at the
beauty in diversity, the beauty of harmony, and learn a
lesson from the vegetable creation. . . . If you meet those
of different race and color from yourself . . . [t]hink of
them as different colored roses growing in the beautiful
garden of humanity, and rejoice to be among them.*

Equality of Women

'Abdu'l-Baha also champions the equality of the sexes; men
and women are both created by God, and "in the estimation of
God, there is no distinction as to male and female." The only
thing that matters is a pure heart. God judges people by their
actions, not by whether they are male or female. Any differences
in the capabilities of women and men, says 'Abdu'l-Baha, are
due entirely to a lack of opportunity and education. Equality of
women is necessary for the progress of humanity. 'Abdu'l-Baha
compares humankind to a bird:

*The world of humanity has two wings—one is women
and the other men. Not until both wings are equally
developed can the bird fly. Should one wing remain
weak, flight is impossible. Not until the world of women
becomes equal to the world of men in the acquisition of
virtues and perfections, can success and prosperity be
attained as they ought to be.*

Economic Matters

'Abdu'l-Baha writes that wealth is not the way to happiness. Economic policies that bring wealth to one person or
nation at the expense of another harm everyone. The fundamen-
tals of economics are ruled by divine principles. They arise out
of the hearts and minds of people and are spiritual in nature.

The Baha'i scriptures advocate voluntary sharing of wealth.
People come closer to God through voluntary good deeds. The rich
should help the poor of their own free will, because it is the right
thing to do, not because they are forced to do it. Freely choosing to
give to others leads to the peace and comfort of society.

Writings of the Bab

Because Baha'is consider their religion to have begun with the Bab, his writings, too, are a part of Baha'i scripture. His principal work, the Bayan, is a book of holy laws. In setting down these laws, the Bab replaces the laws in the Koran. His is clearly a new revelation. The Bab offered new forms of ritual prayer, fasting, and pilgrimage, as well as new forms of tithing, or paying part of one's income to the faith. He also created the 19-month solar calendar, later adapted by Baha'u'llah.

Baha'u'llah based parts of the Aqdas on the Bayan. Much of the Bab's other work was destroyed during the persecution of the Babis. But portions remain, particularly prayers. These are included in Baha'i Prayers.

CHAPTER 5

The Spread of the Baha'i Faith

*F*rom the time Babism was reborn as the Baha'i Faith in 1863, Baha'is actively taught people about the faith. Its leaders sent out believers to spread the word. In its early years, most of the growth of the Baha'i Faith took place in Persia, or Iran, where the faith began. But there were early followers in other countries as well. Parts of the Ottoman Empire, Russia, Egypt, India, and Turkmenistan had Baha'i followers. By the 1880s, still within Baha'u'llah's lifetime, the religion had rebounded from a few hundred Babi survivors to many thousand followers.

The Baha'i Faith in the Ottoman Empire and Egypt

Almost from its beginnings, the Baha'i Faith had small groups of followers in parts of the Ottoman Empire, such as Baghdad, where Baha'u'llah spent part of his exile. There was also a community in Egypt. Mostly these communities were made up of Persians who had moved out of Iran. These groups remained small. They were constantly under threat of arrest and exile. So they did little to spread the faith. In the 1890s in Egypt, however, some native Egyptians converted to the Baha'i Faith, creating a small but devoted community.

British India and Burma

By the 1870s, there was a small network of Baha'is in northern India. At first, it was made up of Indians who had been educated in Persia and had come into contact with the Baha'i Faith there. Later, the Baha'i teacher Sulayman Kahn traveled widely in the area, and the number of converts grew. He then moved to Burma and established a community of Baha'is in that country.

The Baha'i Faith in Russian Territory

The Baha'i Faith established itself early in the Russian territories that shared a border with Persia. The first was Azerbaijan. Babism had taken root in the Persian-controlled area of Azerbaijan when the Bab was in prison there. Beginning in the 1860s, the Babi groups became Baha'is. The religion spread outward into the Russian territories in Azerbaijan and into Ashkhabad, Turkmenistan. Persian immigrants added to its numbers. Then in 1889, some Shi'ah extremists planned and carried out an attack against the Ashkhabad community. To the surprise of the Baha'is, the Russian authorities caught the extremists and put them on trial. They were convicted and put in jail for their crime. This was the first time in Baha'i history that a government had not tolerated persecution directed at Baha'is. The Russian territories became a popular place for Baha'i resettlement, and the community grew.

True to their social mission, the Baha'is in Ashkhabad established schools, a public bath, a hostel, a clinic, and a hospital. In 1907, they built the first Baha'i house of worship. They were probably the first Baha'i community to elect a council. In so doing they became the model for Baha'i communities to come. The Turkmenistan community flourished until the coming of the Communists, who outlawed all religious practice.

The Baha'i Faith in Its Homeland

Persia was the cradle of Babism and later of the Baha'i Faith. From the 1880s on, more and more people there began joining the Baha'i Faith. Many of these new converts were prominent in society. They included Muslim clergy, government officials, and even members of the royal family. They also included members of the Jewish and Zoroastrian faiths. Around this time the religion began to encourage women to become active participants. Wives and daughters joined husbands and fathers. Families began to bring up their children as Baha'is.

From prison in Akka, Baha'u'llah kept up a lively correspondence with his followers. To help in administering the growing faith, he named four leading Baha'is "Hands of the Cause of God." They helped to organize what was becoming an important national movement.

Baha'is in Persia still suffered persecution at the hands of the Muslim clergy and the Persian government. But they followed Baha'u'llah's teachings and deliberately did not fight back. Baha'u'llah urged his followers to avoid politics but to be loyal citizens of their country. Their steadfastness in the face of persecution won them sympathy and more converts.

'Abdu'l-Baha

When Baha'u'llah died in 1892, his eldest son, 'Abdu'l-Baha, became the head of the Baha'i Faith. He was well prepared. During Baha'u'llah's last years, he had turned most of the day-to-day management of the Baha'i movement over to 'Abdu'l-Baha. In his will, Baha'u'llah clearly named 'Abdu'l-Baha as his successor. From 1892 until his death in 1921, 'Abdu'l-Baha was the head of the faith. He furthered Baha'u'llah's vision and shaped the faith in his own way as well. Under 'Abdu'l-Baha, such things as the equality of women, racial equality, education, and economic issues received new and stronger emphasis.

'Abdu'l-Baha was born in 1844, the same year the Bab declared his mission. His birth name was Abbas Effendi, but early in life he took the name 'Abdu'l-Baha, meaning "Servant of Baha." From an early age, he worked as his father's assistant. As a young man in Edirne, he was responsible for Baha'u'llah's large household, which included not only his mother and sister but also his three half brothers and two half sisters, as well as disciples and other family members. He also served as one of his father's secretaries. His father came to rely heavily on him and referred to him as "the Master."

Like his father before him, 'Abdu'l-Baha never attended school. But he read widely, and the Ottoman leaders in Akka respected his scholarship. He married the daughter of a Baha'i merchant in 1873. Together they had seven children, of whom four daughters survived to adulthood. Unlike his father and grandfather, who had followed the Muslim custom of taking several wives, he had only one. Baha'u'llah had stated that taking only one wife was preferred. Under 'Abdu'l-Baha, monogamy became the Baha'i standard.

When Baha'u'llah moved out of Akka, 'Abdu'l-Baha stayed behind. He attended the local mosque, gave to the poor, and prayed regularly. He fit in well with the local Muslim society. However, he was constantly thinking about the faith and how it might develop in the future. In 1875 he wrote *The Secret of Divine Civilization*, which discussed the modernizing of Iran. In 1886, he wrote *A Traveler's Narrative*, a short history of the Baha'i Faith.

Difficulties of Succession

Most Baha'is accepted 'Abdu'l-Baha's authority without question. However, he immediately faced problems within his own family. His half brother, Muhammad-Ali, felt that he himself should have been named leader. In a move that echoed the actions of Mirza Yahya against Baha'u'llah years earlier, he began a campaign to discredit his older brother.

'Abdu'l-Baha's sister, wife, and daughters remained loyal to him, along with an uncle and the uncle's family. But other members of the family sided with Muhammad-Ali. The family infighting did little damage to the loyalty of most followers but it drew the attention of the Turkish authorities to the Baha'is. They reinstated the order of confinement, and 'Abdu'l-Baha was once again a prisoner in Akka.

Muhammad-Ali's opposition only made 'Abdu'l-Baha's own position clearer. 'Abdu'l-Baha advanced the doctrine that Baha'i followers should enter into a sacred covenant that protected Baha'i unity. This covenant required them to be obedient to their appointed leaders. He denounced Muhammad-Ali and his family as "covenant-breakers" for their disloyalty and ousted them from the faith.

The Baha'i Faith Spreads to the West

Americans first heard of Baha'u'llah at the Parliament of the World's Religions, a world religion conference held in Chicago in 1893. At about the same time, a Syrian merchant named Ibrahim Kheiralla immigrated to the United States. A recent convert to the Baha'i Faith, he offered classes in the Baha'i Faith for anyone who was interested. By 1894, a small Baha'i group organized in Chicago. That group grew quickly.

One early American convert was Phoebe Randolph Hearst, mother of the millionaire publisher William Randolph Hearst. In 1898, she gathered a group of Baha'i pilgrims, including Kheiralla, and they traveled to Akka to meet 'Abdu'l-Baha.

'Abdu'l-Baha's personality had a great impact on the Americans. His brilliant mind, his charm, and his spiritual understanding led them to compare him to Jesus Christ of Christianity. Mrs. Hearst, in particular, thought that 'Abdu'l-Baha might be the Messiah. 'Abdu'l-Baha denied this. "No name, no title, no mention, no commendation have I, nor will ever have, except 'Abdu'l-Baha [Servant of Baha]. This is my greatest yearning. This is my eternal life. This is my everlasting glory."

The Hearst party returned to America full of excitement. Their joy and enthusiasm were contagious. In the next few years, a steady stream of visitors poured into Akka. By 1900, there were more Baha'i groups, probably numbering around 1,500 people in all, in the West, with groups located in the United States; Canada; Paris, France; and London, England.

Upheaval in America

Ibrahim Kheiralla had attracted many Americans to the Baha'i Faith. However, his teachings differed widely from those of Baha'is in the Middle East. He went to Akka hoping to get 'Abdu'l-Baha's approval for his version of Baha'i teachings.

Instead, 'Abdu'l-Baha corrected his views and told him to study the Baha'i writings more seriously. Kheiralla refused. He had imagined himself as the leader of the faith in the West. For a time he considered joining ranks with Muhammad-Ali to seize the leadership of the faith from 'Abdu'l-Baha. His attempts to get the American Baha'is to reject 'Abdu'l-Baha's leadership failed, however. Instead, they turned to 'Abdu'l-Baha for guidance. For a short time the struggle over leadership seemed to threaten the Baha'i movement in North America. In the end, however, it emerged stronger and more unified.

The Leadership of 'Abdu'l-Baha

From Akka, 'Abdu'l-Baha continued to direct the faith by letters and through followers across the region. He was an inspired leader. He spoke with great authority about the spiritual and theological aspects of the religion, and his words drew many people to him. He also had a gift for organization. He worked to create the internal structure that would govern the Baha'i Faith. He encouraged Baha'is in different parts of the world to elect local councils.

In 1908, a revolution freed all political prisoners of the Ottoman Empire. 'Abdu'l-Baha was free to leave Akka. He first went to Haifa, where he oversaw the burial of the Bab's remains in a shrine on the slope of Mt. Carmel. This was the place Baha'u'llah himself had chosen. It was also the place where the world center of the faith would be established.

'Abdu'l-Baha was in his sixties, and his health was not good. But for the first time since his childhood, he was not a prisoner. Finally able to travel freely, he began his active ministry. Under his leadership, the faith grew and spread, and many of its doctrines became established.

'Abdu'l-Baha also wrote his will. It would not be made public until after his death. But it was the blueprint for the growth and spread of the Baha'i Faith. In it, he appointed his grandson, Shoghi Effendi, to be the Guardian of the Faith after him. Shoghi Effendi was then only a child. But in him, 'Abdu'l-Baha saw the future of the young religion.

'Abdu'l-Baha's Travels

'Abdu'l-Baha left Palestine in 1910, bound for Egypt. He was still suffering the effects of his long imprisonment. He stayed in Egypt for several months, resting and recuperating. Then in August 1911, he sailed for France. This was the beginning of a journey that took him throughout the Western world.

■ *The Shrine of the Bab, on the slopes of Mt. Carmel, Israel, set among the terraced gardens completed in 2001.*

In the next 28 months, he visited London, England; Paris, France; Stuttgart, Germany; and other European towns and cities as well. Then he sailed for North America.

'Abdu'l-Baha arrived in New York City on April 11, 1912. He traveled the country from coast to coast, visiting more than 40 cities and towns. In Wilmette, Illinois, he laid the cornerstone for the first Baha'i temple in North America. He visited Eliot, Maine, where the Baha'i Faith was presented at the Green Acre retreat. He traveled to Canada and spent time in Montreal.

American and European newspapers gave 'Abdu'l-Baha's travels wide coverage. 'Abdu'l-Baha spoke in churches, universities, peace societies, union halls, and living rooms. It was the first time many Westerners had heard of the Baha'i Faith. For the young Baha'i communities in Europe, Canada, and the United States, it was a wonderful opportunity to meet their leader, listen to his words, and deepen their understanding of both the spiritual and social aspects of the faith. By the end of his tour, there was a whole new wave of Baha'i believers.

The American Baha'i community, small as it was, had a great impact on the growth of the faith. The group moved to translate Baha'i literature into English. They wrote brochures explaining the faith directed at Christian readers. They began to set up local councils and to plan for a yearly national convention. Some members traveled to Persia to help with medical and educational work. Others became missionary teachers. They visited existing communities in such places as Hawaii and Germany. In the next few years, they visited Japan, Australia, and Brazil and established communities there.

World War I

'Abdu'l-Baha returned to Haifa shortly before the beginning of World War I, after more than two years of constant travel. The world situation soon made travel impossible. He turned again to writing letters to his followers. He wrote the *Tablets of the Divine Plan* (1917–1918) to Baha'is in North America. In these letters, he urged his followers to begin a campaign to spread the faith not only in the United States and Canada, but also throughout the world.

'Abdu'l-Baha's Final Years

'Abdu'l-Baha's travels had made him a world figure. He was recognized as the leader of an important religious movement. Following the war, he was able to use his influence to help Palestine when it faced a famine. The British, who had recently taken control of Palestine, made him a knight of the British Empire in 1920.

'Abdu'l-Baha spent his last years in Haifa, directing the work of the Baha'i Faith and corresponding with Baha'i faithful. The faith was now established in many countries around the world, and its followers numbered around 100,000. An active student of world affairs, he warned that the peace accords that had ended World War I would not end conflict and that the Balkan nations would continue to be unstable. Many of his predictions proved to be true. He insisted, however, that they were not divine revelation but simply rational thinking.

'Abdu'l-Baha died on November 28, 1921. His funeral brought together an estimated 10,000 people. They included representatives from the Muslim, Roman Catholic, Greek Orthodox, and Jewish communities of Palestine; also in attendance were the British high commissioner and the governor of Jerusalem. In the 13 years between the end of his confinement as a political prisoner in Akka and his death, he had given the Baha'i Faith world recognition. He had clarified its goals, both spiritual and social. And he had given it an organizational structure that would carry it into the next phase of its existence.

Shoghi Effendi

The terms of 'Abdu'l-Baha's will, which made his grandson Shoghi Effendi the Guardian of the Faith after him, were clear. It named Shoghi Effendi the "sign of God" on Earth and directed Baha'is to be obedient to his direction.

Shoghi Effendi Rabbani was born in 1897. He was the son of 'Abdu'l-Baha's daughter and the oldest of 'Abdu'l-Baha's 13 grandchildren. As a teenager, he spent his summers as his grandfather's assistant. He graduated from college in Beirut, Lebanon, in 1918, and became his grandfather's chief secretary. In 1920, he went to study at Oxford University in England. He wanted to

■ *Shoghi Effendi as a young man.*

improve his English so that he could translate Baha'i scriptures. He was at Oxford when his grandfather died.

Shoghi Effendi Assumes Leadership

Shoghi Effendi was 24 years old when he became leader of the Baha'i Faith. Most Baha'is accepted him gladly as his grandfather's true heir. The young man faced a huge task. 'Abdu'l-Baha had grown old serving the religion. He had seemed like a father to his followers. Shoghi Effendi was young, with modern ideas and a Western education. His leadership would be quite different.

It took several years for Shoghi Effendi to take control of his many new duties. At first he worked day and night, almost to the verge of collapse. Over the course of his 36 years as Guardian, he sent more than 17,500 letters. He kept up with the progress of all the existing Baha'i communities. The situation in the Middle East, where the religion was still under attack, required his response. During this time, he translated a great many of Baha'u'llah's writings into English. His grandfather had dreamed of establishing a world center of the faith in Haifa. It was Shoghi Effendi's job to make that dream a reality.

Shoghi Effendi had a clear vision for the progress of the faith. Two aspects of his leadership were especially important to him. From the beginning of his time as its leader, he focused on developing its administration and on spreading the faith worldwide.

Shoghi Effendi dedicated his life almost entirely to achieving his goals for the Baha'i Faith. Unlike his grandfather, he did not attend the local mosque. He sent representatives to local affairs rather than going himself. Also unlike his grandfather, he did not visit Baha'i communities in other countries. In his many letters, he referred to his position as Guardian, rather than to himself personally.

The Scriptural Canon

One of Shoghi Effendi's greatest contributions to the faith was his interpretation and translation of the works of Baha'u'llah and 'Abdu'l-Baha. His grandfather's will had named him the sole authority for interpreting Baha'i works. Shoghi Effendi was fluent in Persian and Arabic as well as English. His ability to translate the scriptures into English was a major factor in the growth of the American Baha'i community. Over the years of his guardianship, he was the principal translator of most of the Baha'i scriptures. He also wrote an important history of the first hundred years of the Baha'i Faith, *God Passes By*.

The Administrative Plan

Among Shoghi Effendi's many accomplishments as Guardian was his development of a systematic administrative order. The faith had grown too large to be administered by just one person or even one group. He therefore introduced an organizational system. To aid the spiritual assemblies that made up the faith, he introduced requirements for voting, membership rolls, and national centers to administer such matters as translating and publishing. A better network of Baha'i communities emerged.

Shoghi Effendi created an International Baha'i Council to help him in his work. He named a group of devoted believers the "Hands of the Cause of God." Their job was to help the national spiritual assemblies achieve their goals, and to advance and protect the faith. Finally, he established auxiliary boards to assist the Hands.

The Teaching Plan

Once the assemblies were functioning smoothly, Shoghi Effendi turned his attention to teaching. This was to be the principal means for spreading the faith around the world. Under his direction, a seven-year plan (1937–1944) was produced. It called on Baha'is to settle in all the American states, Canadian provinces, and Latin American countries where there were no Baha'is. The Baha'is who undertook this challenge were known as "pioneers." American Baha'is were also to work toward finishing the Baha'i temple at Wilmette, Illinois (near Chicago).

A second seven-year plan (1946–1953) directed Baha'is in North America to continue their work in the Americas. They were also to help Europe recover after World War II and to reestablish the faith there. Other national assemblies received goals as well.

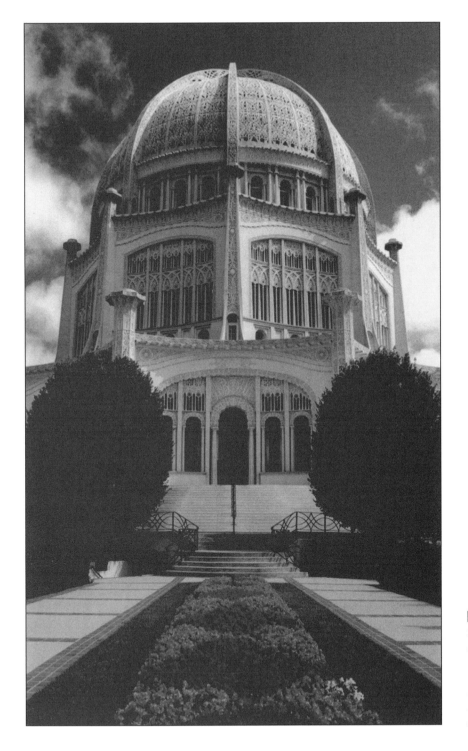

■ 'Abdu'l-Baha laid the cornerstone for the house of worship in Wilmette, Illinois, in 1912 during his visit to America. It was the first Baha'i temple built in the West.

In 1953, Shoghi Effendi launched a 10-year Global Crusade. Its purpose was to establish the faith throughout the world in all the countries where it was not yet established.

The Baha'i World Center

Under Shoghi Effendi, the Baha'i World Center at Haifa, Israel, became a reality. First, he purchased the mansion at Bahji, near Akka, where Baha'u'llah had lived at the end of his life. Later, he purchased more land and created gardens. He did the same with land around the Shrine of the Bab and directed the erection of a golden-domed building over the shrine. He saw to the building of an International Archives Building nearby. In it are kept Baha'i scriptures and relics. He approved a master plan for the development of a center that would eventually be a complex of buildings, gardens, and shrines. It would be the place that Baha'is from all over the world could identify as the center of their religion.

The Hands of the Cause

In 1957, Shoghi Effendi died unexpectedly in London. He had not left a will. 'Abdu'l-Baha had obviously meant the institution of Guardian to be handed down within the family, but Shoghi Effendi and his wife had no children. He had not named a successor. There would be no more Guardians. Nor had he left specific instructions for the direction of the faith after his death. The 10-year plan was only half completed. Shoghi Effendi's death was a serious blow to Baha'is worldwide.

Shortly before his death, however, Shoghi Effendi had named the Hands of the Cause "Chief Stewards" of the faith. He had given them the authority to see that plans for the future were carried out. They therefore took on the responsibility of carrying the faith forward.

Under their stewardship, the faith continued to grow and spread, and Shoghi Effendi's blueprint for a global religion took on substance. The 10-year plan moved forward on schedule, eventually achieving its goals. The Hands of the Cause also took steps toward establishing the Universal House of Justice, to which they handed over their authority in 1963.

Shoghi Effendi's Legacy

Shoghi Effendi worked all his life to spread the faith throughout the world. To a large extent, he succeeded. The plans he initiated exceeded their goals. In 1935, before the first plan, there were 139 spiritual assemblies worldwide, and Baha'is lived in 1,034 localities. By 1953, those numbers had increased to 670 spiritual assemblies and 2,700 localities.

Shoghi Effendi did not live to see the completion of his 10-year crusade. But his plan vastly increased the Baha'i Faith's geographical presence in the world. By 1963, Baha'i had 4,437 spiritual assemblies and was established in 14,437 localities. The number of national assemblies increased from 10 in 1935 to 56 in 1963. During Shoghi Effendi's time as Guardian, the number of people professing the Baha'i Faith had reached more than 400,000. In the next half-century, it would grow even more.

CHAPTER 6

Baha'i Belief
and Worship

Baha'i worship has few formal structures. There are no priests, ministers, mullahs, or rabbis. There is no liturgy, and there are no rituals. As in most other areas of the religion, a great deal is left up to the individual. Baha'is guide themselves along the path that leads them to spiritual truth. The whole of Baha'i life is a spiritual quest.

The Spiritual Journey

Baha'u'llah writes that all creation reflects divine attributes. Yet of all creation, human beings are special. Only humans can reflect all of the attributes of God. "Alone of all created things, man hath been singled out for so great a favor, so enduring a bounty," says Baha'u'llah. Human lives have two aspects, he says—the material or animal side and the spiritual side; what makes a person truly human is his or her spiritual nature.

According to Baha'u'llah, people cannot find true happiness in worldly things: "The world is but a show, vain and empty, a mere nothing, bearing the semblance of reality." He tells his followers that instead of grasping at material things, they must try to develop the divine power within them. At the same time, people

are not to deny themselves the good things of the world in the name of religion. The goal is moderation and thankfulness, not extreme self-denial. In *Gleanings*, Baha'u'llah writes:

> Should a man wish to adorn himself with the ornaments of the earth, to wear its apparels, or partake of the bene-fits it can bestow, no harm can befall him, if he alloweth nothing whatever to intervene between him and God, for God hath ordained every good thing, whether created in the heavens or in the earth, for such of his servants as truly believe in Him. Eat ye, O people, of the good things which God hath allowed you, and deprive not yourself from his wondrous bounties. Render thanks and praise unto him, and be of them that are truly thankful.

Divine Attributes

What attributes give humans spiritual power? According to Baha'u'llah, they include justice, love, trustworthiness and truthfulness, purity and chastity, actions, and service to others. People who seek to develop these qualities within themselves are following a spiritual path.

Justice and Love

Baha'u'llah particularly stresses the importance of justice. Baha'is must always be just and even-handed in their treatment of others and respect the rights of all. They should also show the same fairness to themselves. "Be fair to yourselves and to others, that the evidences of justice may be revealed, through your deeds, among Our faithful servants," he says.

Love is also very important. 'Abdu'l-Baha points out that there are many kinds of love: love of family, of country, of institutions, of one's own race. However, all of these are imperfect. In loving their own country, for example, some people may find fault with other countries. True spiritual love is universal and unlimited. It reaches out to everyone. Baha'u'llah also praises other qualities that grow out of love for humanity. These qualities include kindness, friendliness, compassion, consideration, patience, and generosity.

> ■ *The best beloved of all things in My sight is Justice; turn not away there from if thou desirest Me, and neglect it not that I may confide in thee. By its aid though shalt see with thine own eyes and not through the eyes of others, and shalt know of thine own knowledge and not through the knowledge of thy neighbor. Ponder this in thy heart; how it behooveth thee to be. Verily [truly] justice is my gift to thee and the sign of my loving-kindness. Set it then before thine eyes.*
>
> —From ***Arabic Hidden Words, 2***

Trustworthiness

According to Baha'i scripture, trustworthiness is the basis of all human interaction. Without trustworthiness, people cannot truly conduct the business of life. Prosperity is built on trust. Along with this goes truthfulness, which 'Abdu'l-Baha calls "the foundation of all human virtues." A truthful person is always sincere and deals honestly with others.

Purity and Chastity

Purity and chastity are required of all Baha'is. However, they are warned not to become puritanical or self-denying. They should strive for moderation in matters of dress, language, and amusements. They should be modest, pure, and temperate, and should keep their thoughts pure. They are to be chaste but not prudish. And they should develop habits that safeguard their health. Baha'is are discouraged from smoking and are forbidden to use alcohol or mind-altering drugs unless prescribed by a physician for a medical condition.

Work and Service

"Let deeds, not words, be your adorning," Baha'u'llah writes. "The essence of faith is fewness of words and abundance of deeds." One way that Baha'is show their faith is in service to others. Baha'is donate their time to teaching or community projects. In the Baha'i Faith, it is a duty to have a trade or profession. Baha'is are asked to use their skills to enrich both their own lives and the lives of those around them. Work is a form of worship.

Baha'i Laws

To Baha'is, discipline is an essential part of reaching any goal, and spiritual progress requires spiritual discipline. Baha'u'llah offered his followers a number of laws to help them work toward unity and harmony. Among these laws are social laws, such as the laws for marriage, and obligations for achieving spiritual growth. These include prayer, reading of scriptures, meditation, and fasting.

Prayer and Meditation

Prayer is one of the most important obligations of a Baha'i. Every Baha'i is expected to pray daily and to meditate. Baha'is may create their own prayers, or they may use any of the many prayers written by the Bab, Baha'u'llah, and 'Abdu'l-Baha, which have been translated into many languages. The only requirement is that one of the daily prayers must come from the obligatory prayers of Baha'u'llah.

There are three obligatory prayers. A Baha'i may choose any one of them. The "Short Obligatory Prayer" is one such prayer; it is to be said sometime between noon and sunset:

> *I bear witness, O my God, that Thou has created me to know Thee and to worship Thee. I testify, at this moment, to my powerlessness and to Thy might, to my poverty and to Thy wealth.*
>
> *There is none other God but Thee, the Help in Peril, the Self-Subsisting.*

Prayers may be spoken, chanted, or even sung. Baha'u'llah approved of music, and according to 'Abdu'l-Baha, "The art of music is divine and effective. It is the food of the soul and spirit." Baha'i hymns are words from the scriptures set to music.

Baha'u'llah also instructs his followers to read scripture and to meditate. This duty requires them to read from the scriptures twice a day, morning and evening, and to think about the essential meaning. The act of meditating helps to turn the individual's mind away from the world and toward spiritual things. According to 'Abdu'l-Baha, "When you meditate you are speaking with your own spirit. In that state of mind you put certain questions to your spirit and the spirit answers: the light breaks forth and the reality is revealed."

Fasting

Another Baha'i obligation is fasting. During the Baha'i month of Ala, from March 2 to March 20, Baha'is fast from sunrise to sunset, as Muslims do during the holy month of Ramadan. This is a time of spiritual preparation for the New Year, which begins on March 21. According to Shoghi Effendi, the fast is a period of meditation and prayer that leads to spiritual renewal. The Baha'i fast is a symbol of the need to turn away from things of the world and toward God.

Marriage

In the Baha'i Faith, marriage is recommended, although not required. According to 'Abdu'l-Baha, "Baha'i marriage is the commitment of the two parties one to the other, and their mutual attachment of mind and heart." The Baha'i Faith recognizes the importance of the physical bond of marriage but stresses that the spiritual side is more important. Since the time of 'Abdu'l-Baha's leadership, monogamy between a man and a woman is the only form of marriage permitted. Baha'is consider the institution of marriage to be God-given and vital to society.

The Baha'i Faith requires that both the man and the woman consent freely to the marriage, as must their parents. 'Abdu'l-Baha emphasizes the importance of the couple's knowing each other well. They should "exercise the utmost care to become thoroughly acquainted with the character of the other. . . .Their purpose must be this: to become loving companions and comrades and at one with each other for time and eternity."

The marriage ceremony has no set form. Couples may write their own service. They may incorporate any local customs they wish. The only set part of the ceremony is that they must exchange a vow before witnesses. That vow is, "We will all, verily, abide by the Will of God."

Divorce is strongly discouraged. However, it may be permitted as a last resort after a year of separation and attempts to reconcile. If the couple still cannot agree, permission to divorce is granted.

■ Baha'i children learn about their faith from an early age. These girls and their teacher are discussing the meaning and importance of the Baha'i feast.

Family Life and Children

Baha'is place great emphasis on the importance of family. The family is the source of spiritual growth for the individual. It is also the foundation of society. The family provides a spiritual atmosphere for children to grow and learn. The education of children is central to Baha'i belief.

The Baha'i Faith teaches that the most important social function of marriage is that of raising children. Parents are to create an atmosphere of love and harmony in their home. In such an atmosphere, all members of the family can flourish. Parents must set the example for their children. They must be truthful, free of prejudice, and just. In their relationship with each other, they must demonstrate the equality of men and women.

Baha'is recognize three kinds of education. Physical education provides the skills that enable people to survive. Education in reading and writing, arts and sciences, allows people to participate in the world and to enjoy the benefits of knowledge. Spiritual education makes individuals complete human beings.

Education of children is a religious duty in the Baha'i Faith. Education begins at, or even before, birth, as parents prepare themselves to bring up their children according to Baha'i teachings. A child's early years are the most important in developing good character. "While the branch is green and tender, it can easily be made straight," writes 'Abdu'l-Baha. When children are old enough, they should go to school. Baha'i writings especially stress the importance of educating girls, because they will be the first teachers of the next generation.

'Abdu'l-Baha says that parents must tend their children as a gardener tends tender young plants, seeing that they grow strong in faith. Parents should applaud and praise their good deeds and qualities and punish their misdeeds if necessary. However, punishment is to be based on reason. It is never permitted to strike or belittle a child, as these things damage the child's character. Children are the future and hope of the world. They must always be treated with respect and dignity.

The Covenant

The Baha'i Faith does not ask its members to follow any specific creed or doctrine. Every Baha'i has the freedom to read and interpret the scriptures for him- or herself. But all Baha'is live by a single unifying principle. This is the Covenant, or Baha'i spiritual agreement.

The Covenant is the unifying force that holds the Baha'i Faith together. "The power of the Covenant will protect the Cause of Baha'u'llah from the doubts of the people of error," wrote 'Abdu'l-Baha. "It is the fortified fortress of the cause of God and the firm pillar of the religion of God. Today no power can conserve the oneness of the Baha'i world save the Covenant of God."

The Covenant leaves each follower of the Baha'i Faith free to interpret the scriptures. At the same time, it prohibits any individual from claiming that his or hers is the only correct interpretation. Only the writings of Baha'u'llah and the interpretations of 'Abdu'l-Baha and Shoghi Effendi are authoritative.

People become Baha'is by agreeing to abide by the Covenant. There is no conversion ceremony for those joining from another faith, and no other requirement. Similarly, there is no confirmation ceremony. When young people reach the age of 15, which is considered the age of consent, they may choose to join the fellowship. They simply agree to abide by Baha'i laws and are admitted to the community.

Death and Burial

In the Baha'i Faith, death marks the point at which the soul passes to the next world. As such, it is "the bearer of gladness" for the believer, according to Baha'u'llah. There is no way to prove that there is life after death. However, Baha'is believe that life does not end with death; the soul is eternal. 'Abdu'l-Baha writes, "To consider that after the death of the body the spirit perishes is like imagining that a bird in a cage will be destroyed if the cage is broken, though the bird has nothing to fear from the destruction of the cage."

As the vessel that has housed the soul during life, the body is treated with respect. Funeral ceremonies are dignified. There is a specific prayer for funerals. Otherwise, the ceremony may be as simple or elaborate as the family wishes. Cremation is forbidden. Bodies are buried so that they may naturally become part of the earth. Baha'i laws require that Baha'is be buried within an hour's journey of the place of death.

The Baha'i Faith teaches that believers can help those who have died in the next world. They can do this by performing good deeds in their name or through prayer.

■ **Prayer of Intercession for the Dead**

O my God! Thou forgiver of sins, bestower of gifts, dispeller of afflictions!

Verily, I beseech Thee to forgive the sins of such as have abandoned the physical garment and have ascended to the spiritual world. O my Lord! Purify them from trespasses, dispel their sorrows, and change their darkness into light. Cause them to enter the garden of happiness, cleanse them with the most pure water, and grant them to behold Thy splendors on the loftiest mount.

—'Abdu'l-Baha, **Baha'i Prayers**

The Baha'i Calendar

All of the world's calendars are associated in some way with religion. The calendar the secular world uses is actually the Christian calendar, which begins with the birth of Jesus Christ. But there are also Jewish and Islamic calendars that date from important events in those religions. Baha'i religious life is organized around a solar calendar originally developed by the Bab and adapted by Baha'u'llah.

The Baha'i year begins with the spring equinox, March 21, which was the traditional New Year's Day in Iran. The months are named after spiritual or divine qualities.

Each year has 19 months of 19 days. In order to bring the number of days to 365, four additional days are inserted before the last month of the year. These days are called Ayyam-i-Ha. Baha'is celebrate this time by inviting others to their homes for

Baha'i Month	Translation	Begins
Baha	Splendor	March 21
Jalal	Glory	April 9
Jamal	Beauty	April 28
Azamaat	Grandeur	May 17
Nur	Light	June 5
Rahmat	Mercy	June 24
Kalimat	Words	July 13
Kamal	Perfection	August 1
Asma	Names	August 20
Izzat	Might	September 8
Mashiyyat	Will	September 27
Ilm	Knowledge	October 16
Qudrat	Power	November 4
Qawl	Speech	November 23
Masa'il	Questions	December 12
Sharaf	Honor	December 31
Sultan	Sovereignty	January 19
Mulk	Dominion	February 7
Ala	Loftiness	March 2

Ayyam-i-Ha parties and by giving gifts, visting the sick, and performing community service.

The Nineteen-Day Feast

Every 19 days, at the beginning of each Baha'i month, is a Nineteen-Day Feast. If possible, all Baha'is attend. The feast is the cornerstone of each local Baha'i community activity.

The feast is actually a meeting with three parts. The first part of the meeting is devoted to prayers and the reading of scripture. This is the Baha'i worship service. The second part is an administrative session. People give reports on Baha'i activities in the area. Individuals raise issues that are important to them, and the members of the community discuss them. Finally

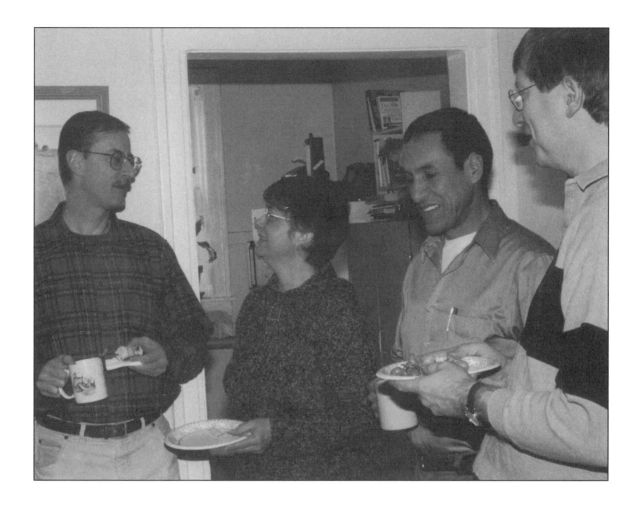

there are refreshments. In smaller communities, the Nineteen Day Feast is held in someone's home. In larger areas, it may be held in the Baha'i centers.

In some places, Baha'is meet weekly for devotions and fellowship. They usually meet on Sundays, when most people do not have to work. Weekly devotions consist of reading from the works of Baha'u'llah or other founders and reciting prayers.

Baha'i Holy Days

Baha'is observe nine holy days, which commemorate events in Baha'i history. Feasts such as Naw-Ruz and Ridvan are celebrations. Baha'is gather to read scripture, consult, and share

The social part of the Nineteen Day Feast helps to strengthen the bonds of love and fellowship in the community.

Baha'i Holy Days	
Naw-Ruz (New Year)	March 21
Ridvan (first day)	April 21
Ridvan (ninth day)	April 29
Ridvan (twelfth day)	May 2
The Bab's Declaration	May 23
Passing of Baha'u'llah	May 29
Martyrdom of the Bab	July 9
Birth of the Bab	October 20
Birth of Baha'u'llah	November 12

fellowship. During Ridvan, the "Most Great Festival," they also elect new leaders. The Passing of Baha'u'llah and the Bab's martyrdom are solemn occasions when Baha'is pray and read scriptures. If possible, they abstain from work on their holy days.

Houses of Worship

Most Baha'i services take place in homes or in Baha'i centers. However, Baha'i houses of worship are a very important part of the Baha'i Faith. Houses of worship are called Mashriqu'l-Adhkar, or "Dawning Place of the Praises of God." At the present time, there are seven houses of worship worldwide. They are in Wilmette, Illinois, as well as New Delhi, India; Kampala, Uganda; Sydney, Australia; Frankfurt, Germany; Panama City, Panama; and Apia, Samoa.

Houses of worship are open for devotional services that people of all religions—or no religious background—may attend. Services are nondenominational. They consist only of readings and prayers from all of the world's religions. Some of these have been set to music and may be sung by a choir. There are no sermons.

All Baha'i houses of worship have nine sides and a dome. These architectural features are symbols that the Baha'i Faith is open to all religious traditions. They show that people may come through many doors, but gather in recognition of one God.

The Baha'i house of worship outside Sidney, Australia, is the first Baha'i temple built in the South Pacific. It was dedicated in September 1961.

In addition to the existing houses of worship, the faith owns property in other countries around the world, where it will eventually build other houses of worship. In time, Baha'is envision that the Mashriqu'l-Adhkars will be the centers of community life. Around them they will build administrative centers, schools, colleges, clinics, homes for the elderly, and other community services. In this way, the house of worship will be the central focus of communities that come together in harmony and service to God.

CHAPTER 7

The Baha'i Community

*T*he Baha'i Faith is organized around the Baha'i community. In the community, Baha'is put their faith into practical action. Through the community, Baha'is implement the social, educational, and spiritual goals of their religion.

The Baha'i Administrative Order

The laws and rules of the Baha'i Faith and Baha'i institutions together form the "Baha'i Administrative Order." The Administrative Order is the way that the Baha'i Faith is organized. To Baha'is, however, it is much more than a system of organization. Its foundations and guiding principles were laid down by its founders; it is therefore sacred. Baha'is understand that the institutional framework of their faith puts words into actions, a central aim of the faith.

Moreover, Baha'is believe that the structure of their religion will eventually develop into a world order. All people and countries, all races and religions will be united as one within the Administrative Order of the Baha'i Faith. Baha'is therefore work diligently to support it and follow its rules, as the best hope for bringing peace and prosperity to all humanity.

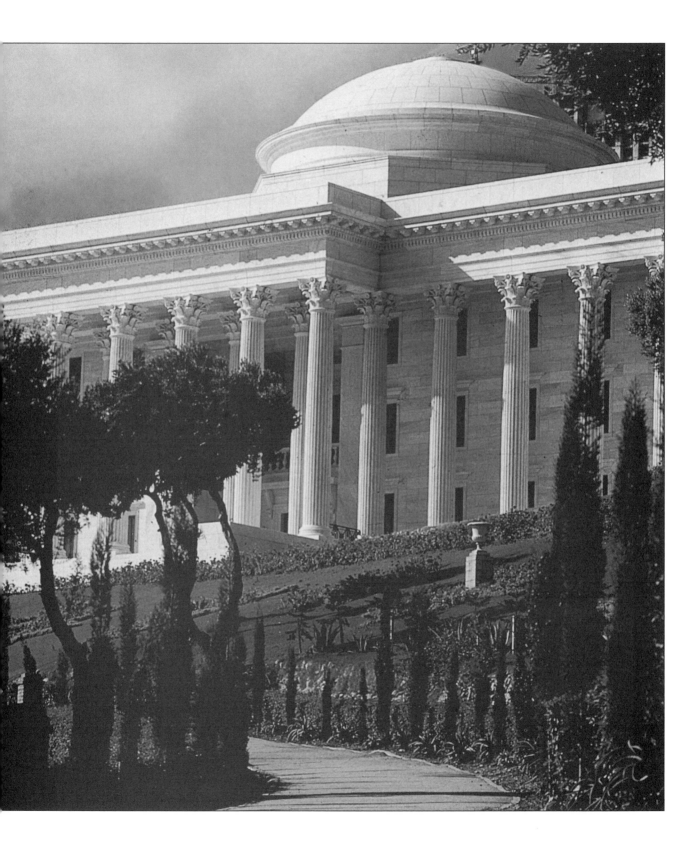

Baha'i Institutions

Preceding page-
The Universal House
of Justice at the Baha'i
World Center in Haifa,
Israel. Its members,
elected by all the
national assemblies,
are the highest authority
in the Baha'i world.

Unlike most other organized religions, such as Judaism, Christianity, and Islam, the Baha'i Faith has no priests or clergy. It has no professional religious scholars who interpret the scriptures for believers. Baha'u'llah taught that a priesthood or clergy was not necessary. In earlier times, when few people could read and write, they needed a professional priesthood. They needed someone who could tell them what the Bible or the Koran said and help them to understand scripture. But the Baha'i Faith is a religion for the modern age. Modern society can give everyone the opportunity to read and write. This means that people can read and understand the scriptures for themselves; a mature humanity does not need a professional clergy.

However, in most organized religions, religious professionals have another important function. They administer the business of the religious body. They coordinate its local, regional, national, and international activities. They serve as a resource for religious matters. Many have publishing houses that produce literature for and about the religion. Others have business offices that oversee mission efforts or schools. In the Baha'i Faith, the administrative structure performs these functions.

The Spiritual Assemblies

Whenever an area has at least nine adult Baha'i members, those nine or more people hold an annual election for the local spiritual assembly, the governing body for the faith in that area. It is responsible for supervising the activities of the faith. Its duties include spreading the word about the Baha'i Faith, running its educational programs, local publicity and publishing, holding devotional services and meetings, finances, and counseling on matters of faith.

A country with a sufficient number of local spiritual assemblies may form a national spiritual assembly. Elected delegates attend an annual convention at which the national spiritual assembly is elected. National spiritual assemblies oversee and coordinate the activities of the local assemblies.

Baha'is hold yearly elections in April during the Festival of Ridvan. All voting is by secret ballot. Baha'i rules prohibit nominations or campaigning. Each member simply lists nine names on his or her ballot. When the ballots are counted, the nine individuals with the highest number of votes are elected to the assembly. Their term begins immediately after the election, and they serve for one full year.

A Baha'i election in Thailand. Elections are held each year during the Festival of Ridvan.

The teachings of Baha'u'llah ask Baha'is to consider the qualities of the people they elect and to choose "only those who can best combine the necessary qualities of unquestioned loyalty, of selfless devotion, of a well-trained mind, of recognized ability and mature experience." However, Baha'u'llah encouraged his followers to give preference to minority members.

The Universal House of Justice

The Universal House of Justice is the international governing body of the Baha'i Faith and the highest authority in the Baha'i world. It has authority for guarding and developing the faith. This authority was handed down directly from

Baha'u'llah. It has the power to set up rules for the Baha'i community and to rule on religious matters not covered in the writings of Baha'u'llah, 'Abdu'l-Baha, or Shoghi Effendi. It is located in Haifa, Israel.

Baha'u'llah himself had left instructions for creating the Universal House of Justice. His plans were later developed by 'Abdu'l-Baha and Shoghi Effendi. The Universal House of Justice finally came into being during the Baha'i World Congress in 1963, when the first members were elected. Members of the Universal House of Justice are elected by the members of all the national assemblies for five-year terms.

The responsibilities of the Universal House of Justice are similar to those of the local and national spiritual assemblies. In addition, they work to

- promote peace among nations
- ensure that no organization within the Baha'i community abuses its privileges
- safeguard the rights of individuals within the Baha'i Faith

- develop the Baha'i World Center and its administrative processes
- resolve disputes within the Baha'i World Center
- preserve the Baha'i Faith's sacred texts

An important function of the Universal House of Justice is the growth and development of the faith around the world. Since it began, it has produced several plans for spreading the faith. These have been the Nine-Year Plan (1964–1973); the Five-Year Plan (1974–79); the Seven-Year Plan (1979–86); the Six-Year Plan (1986–92); the Three-Year Plan (1993–97); the Four-Year Plan (1996–2000); the Twelve-Month Plan (2000–2001); and the Five-Year Plan (2001–2006). The plans are crucial to Baha'i administration, because they set the goals for the spreading of the faith.

The goals of the different plans have included

- spreading the faith around the world and increasing its membership
- establishing and improving the functioning of the Baha'i administrative order in all parts of the world and helping local communities to take on more responsibility for reaching Baha'i goals
- encouraging the individual spiritual development of all Baha'is as well as their participation in all aspects of the Baha'i community
- improving the quality of Baha'i community and family life, especially education
- increasing the involvement of Baha'is in society, particularly with regard to social and economic development
- increasing the translation, production, distribution, and use of Baha'i literature
- spreading the message of Baha'u'llah to all parts of society and all minority groups
- developing the Baha'i World Center
- building new houses of worship
- working with international organizations such as the United Nations and its divisions

All Baha'is must follow the decisions of the Universal House of Justice. However, any decision may be amended at a later time by another ruling. In this way, the faith can grow and change with new times and circumstances.

> ■ *The men of God's House of Justice have been charged with the affairs of the people. They, in truth, are the Trustees of God among his servants and the daysprings of authority in His countries....Inasmuch as for each day there is a new problem and for every problem an expedient solution, such affairs should be referred to the Ministers of the House of Justice that they may act according to the needs and requirements of the time. . . . It is incumbent upon all to be obedient unto them.*
> —Baha'u'llah, **Tablets of Baha'u'llah**

The Baha'i World Center

The Baha'i World Center is in Haifa, Israel. It contains one of the holiest shrines of the Baha'i Faith, the Shrine of the Bab, and also its important administrative buildings. These include:

- The Seat of the Universal House of Justice
- The International Teaching Center
- The International Baha'i Archives
- The Center for the Study of the Texts

The World Center includes the Shrine of the Bab, which houses the Bab's remains. Baha'u'llah himself chose the site of the Bab's shrine on the slope of Mt. Carmel, which he called the "mountain of God." 'Abdu'l-Baha is also buried there. The houses and grounds where the central figures of the Baha'i Faith lived are nearby. They have been restored and are open to Baha'i pilgrims. Baha'i holy places also include the Shrine of Baha'u'llah at Bahji, just outside Akka, and the mansion where Baha'u'llah spent his last years. The Shrine of the Bab, the mansion at Bahji, and the complex of administrative buildings are surrounded by carefully tended gardens. The World Center complex has luxuriant gardens, streams, and fountains on 19 terraces. The World Center is a place of pilgrimage for Baha'is from around the world.

The World Center continues to develop in the 21st century. In 2001, new gardens opened at the Shrine of the Bab and became a major tourist attraction. A Baha'i library is also planned.

■ *The International Archives Building at the World Center in Haifa houses Baha'i relics and scriptures.*

The Baha'i Administrative Institutions

Elected Institutions   **Appointed Institutions**

Universal House of Justice

National Spiritual Assemblies   International Teaching Center

Regional Baha'i Councils   Continental Boards of Counselors

Local Spiritual Assemblies   Auxiliary Board Members

Appointed Institutions

Besides the Baha'i Faith's elected institutions, there are appointed positions. These mostly operate out of the International Teaching Center in Haifa, Israel.

Because no further Hands of the Cause could be appointed after Shoghi Effendi's death, the Universal House of Justice created the International Teaching Center in 1973. The job of the International Teaching Center is to coordinate the Continental Boards of Counselors in promoting and protecting the faith. It also assists the Universal House of Justice in creating its long-term plans. Members are appointed for five-year terms.

The Rights of Minorities

In the words of 'Abdu'l-Baha, "In the estimation of God, all men are equal. There is no distinction of preference for any soul, in the realm of His justice and equity. . . . This variety in forms and coloring, which is manifest in all the kingdoms, is according to creative wisdom and hath a divine purpose." All forms of prejudice are expressly forbidden.

As an article of their faith, Baha'is work to see that the rights of all minorities are protected. Shoghi Effendi wrote,

"Every organized community enlisted under the banner of Baha'u'llah should feel it to be its first and inescapable obligation to nurture, encourage, and safeguard every minority belonging to any faith, race, class, or nation within it."

Consultation

Key to carrying out the Baha'i Administrative Order is the process of consultation. Consultation involves a frank and honest but loving exchange of opinions by members of a group. The goal of consultation is to achieve complete agreement. The result is the fruit of the group's collective wisdom. All decisions in the Baha'i Faith are made by consultation.

When Baha'is come together for consultation, they must do so in the spirit of love and harmony, according to the writings of 'Abdu'l-Baha. He continues:

They must then proceed with the utmost devotion, courtesy, dignity, care and moderation to express their views. They must in every matter search out the truth and not insist upon their own opinion, for stubbornness and persistence in one's views will lead ultimately to discord and wrangling and the truth will remain hidden. The honored members must with all freedom express their own thoughts, and it is in no wise permitted for one to belittle the thought of another, nay, he must with moderation set forth the truth, and should differences of opinion arise, a majority of voices must prevail, and all must obey and submit to the majority.

As Baha'is carry out consultation, however, the goal is not to find a majority opinion. It is to find a unanimous one. If there is no unanimous decision, the majority opinion must be respected. The idea of consensus carries over into all aspects of Baha'i life. It is a tool not only within the Baha'i community but also in school, family, and the workplace.

Power and Authority

In the Baha'i Faith, institutions, not individuals, receive power and authority. An individual who is elected to a position

■ *A local spiritual assembly in Johannesburg, South Africa, meets for consultation.*

in a local or national spiritual assembly does not have any special power and does not consider him- or herself to be a "leader of the Baha'i community." The institution is the leader. It, not the individuals in it, hold the power.

As much as possible, Baha'i institutions pass authority down to the next level, toward the local assemblies, rather than keeping control themselves. For example, it is the responsibility of the Universal House of Justice to see that the faith advances and expands. But as soon as a national assembly has enough experience, it takes over that responsibility in its area. When a local assembly is strong enough, the national assembly encourages it to take over that function. In this way, all individual Baha'is share the power and authority of the faith. Baha'is rely on the Administrative Order and the institutions of the Baha'i Faith to give form and structure to their communities and their daily lives.

Baha'is and Their Community

The institutions of the Baha'i Faith support and sustain the Baha'i community as a whole. Worship, service, teaching, and fellowship all take place within the structure of the Administrative Order. Baha'is understand that in becoming members of the Baha'i Faith, they have joined a community, not merely a congregation. As members of a community, they have an obligation to work together, to support one another, and to do all that they can to help the community thrive. No matter how small their local communities may be, Baha'is also understand that they are part of a worldwide community of believers that stretches around the globe, held together by the sacred laws and institutions of their faith.

CHAPTER **8**

The Baha'i Faith Today

*I*n 1992, 100 years after the passing of Baha'u'llah, Baha'is from around the world met for the Second Baha'i World Congress. An estimated 30,000 Baha'is gathered in New York City for four days. New York, "the City of the Covenant," was where Western audiences first heard 'Abdu'l-Baha proclaim the Covenant of Baha'u'llah on his North American tour in 1912. The Baha'is who gathered there in 1992 were the largest and most diverse group ever to come together in one place.

Satellite links broadcast the conference to groups meeting in Buenos Aires, Argentina; Sidney, Australia; New Delhi, India; Nairobi, Kenya; Panama City, Panama; Bucharest, Hungary; Moscow, Russia; Singapore; and Western Samoa. A highlight of the conference was the participation of the Russian Baha'is. After decades of suppression, the Russian Baha'i community, one of the earliest, has been rebounding since the fall of the Soviet Union.

The members of the Universal House of Justice spoke to the wide-flung conferences from their center in Haifa, Israel. The conference celebrated the growth of the faith and the unity in diversity made possible by the Baha'i Covenant.

Spreading the Faith

The largest Baha'i communities are now in South Asia, Africa, and Latin America. Wherever they have gone, Baha'is have established educational, agricultural, and community development projects. Their concern for social ethics, race relationships, feminist issues, economics, global government, ecology, and law has made the faith attractive to people in underdeveloped areas as well as to those struggling with such issues in some of the most developed countries of the world.

The growth and spread of the Baha'i Faith to different countries generally occurs through what the Baha'is call "pioneering." Pioneers are ordinary Baha'i believers who move to new places and settle there. In their new communities, they find jobs and may buy or rent homes, and educate their children. They may have to learn a new language.

Baha'i pioneers perform missionary service, but they are not professional missionaries. They are not paid by the faith for their work. They support themselves with their trades or professions. They teach and offer other Baha'i services in their free time. Baha'is are forbidden to proselytize—that is, to actively try to convert people of other faiths. They treat believers of other religions with respect and friendship.

■ **Growth in the Institutions of the Baha'i Faith**

	1954	1963	1968	1973	1979	1988	1994	2001
National Spiritual Assemblies	12	56	81	113	125	149	172	182
Local Spiritual Assemblies	708	3,379	5,902	17,037	23,634	19,486*	17,780*	11,740*
Localities where Baha'is Reside	3,117	11,092	31,883	69,541	102,704	112,137	119,276	127,381

*The drop in the number of local spiritual assemblies, beginning in 1979 to the present, is due to reorganizations in which local assemblies have been consolidated to take in more than one town or village.

Firesides

If people show an interest in the Baha'i Faith, they may be invited to a "fireside." These are small study groups that meet in private homes. Baha'is invite friends and neighbors to talk about the faith in an informal setting. They answer questions and discuss their own beliefs and spiritual journeys. Many people around the world have come into the faith through firesides.

■ *Firesides give people who are interested in learning more about the Baha'i Faith a chance to do so in an informal setting.*

Teaching

Education is a central Baha'i value, and teaching is an important Baha'i activity. Both Baha'u'llah and 'Abdu'l-Baha emphasized the importance of education. Because a child's first teacher is usually its mother, both leaders told followers that if they could not afford to educate all their children, they should educate the girls, the mothers of the next generation.

■ Girls work in a greenhouse at the Mongolian Development Center. This Baha'i-inspired project offers health and nutrition programs as well as training in growing essential vegetables.

Currently in the United States, education is one of the most important goals of the faith. The education plan calls on assemblies to establish children's classes that are open to all children, to make the Baha'i Faith a religion of learners. It calls for a network of permanent schools, regional schools, study circles, and after-school programs across the nation. The schools offer such services as homework tutoring, physical education and dance, and the arts.

An important feature of Baha'i teaching is spiritual education. Baha'is believe that the spiritual education of children is the future of the Baha'i Faith. They stress that learning must not end with words, but with service. Children learn the importance of kindness, generosity, compassion, and caring for each other. They learn that through these values and behaviors, they can contribute now as helpers and healers of society.

Development Efforts

Today, Baha'i communities run more than 1,300 local development projects around the world. These include schools, adult literacy programs, health clinics, environmental centers, youth programs, women's programs, agriculture, and vocational training centers. Most of these projects are undertaken in the developing countries.

Baha'is see their social programs as a way to put their faith into action. They believe that social action arises from the best part of the human spirit, and so it is really a spiritual activity. They also see many problems as interconnected. For example, they believe that poverty cannot be eliminated until women have full equality, since most of the world's poor are women and children.

In Baha'i-run programs in rural India, women in vocational training programs learn marketable skills, such as sewing. They also receive instruction in literacy and hygiene. In parts of South America, some poor farmers learn modern methods of farming, and others plant trees to restore forests. Others benefit from day care centers, orphanages, and literacy programs. In a city setting, a new vocational institute offers courses in business management, environmental technology, and nutrition.

In Africa, Baha'is have established a network of health care centers, training villagers in simple techniques of first aid and treatment of common illnesses, such as malaria and infant diarrhea, which are often fatal if untreated. The centers enable people to improve the health and well-being of their communities.

But Baha'is never teach only skills; they teach Baha'i principles as well. They teach consultation techniques so people can arrive at group decisions that benefit the whole community. Students come to understand the oneness of humanity, giving and sharing, honesty, trustworthiness, and service. They see that education is knowledge and that knowledge is power. Students go home with new ideas that make a difference to the entire community. They may or may not become Baha'is, but the Baha'i principles they learn help them to make their communities a better place to live.

The Baha'i Faith and the United Nations

Under Shoghi Effendi, the Baha'i leadership actively encouraged contacts with the United Nations. Many of the UN's goals in such areas as world peace, education, and economic development parallel those of the Baha'i Faith. Leaders saw ways that the two groups could work together. In response, the Universal House of Justice created the Baha'i International Community (BIC).

The Baha'i International Community is registered with the UN as an accredited nongovernmental organization. It has representatives based in Haifa and in New York, Geneva, Paris, Hong Kong, London, Jerusalem, and Fiji. These offices work on projects that promote peace building, human rights, education, health care, the environment, women's equality, and economic development. The BIC calls on national and local Baha'i communities to help in these efforts.

The Universal House of Justice encourages Baha'i support of UN projects. In 1967, Baha'is established a permanent office at the UN in New York City. They consult on the Economic and Social Council and the Children's Fund (UNICEF). They also work with the World Health Organization (WHO) and the UN Environment Program (UNEP).

The Baha'i International Community has been affiliated with the United Nations since 1948.

Persecution in Recent Times

Throughout the 20th century, Baha'is have continued to undergo systematic persecution. In Nazi Germany, the faith was officially banned. The Baha'i teaching that all races are fundamentally one was contrary to Nazi doctrine. When communism took over the Soviet Union, Baha'is were not permitted to practice their faith. The first Baha'i house of worship, built in Ishqabad in the 19th century, was confiscated and eventually torn down. Many Russian Baha'is were exiled to Siberia for continuing their religious activities. But as with other religions under communism, the Baha'i community has begun to rebound since the breakup of the Soviet Union.

In the Middle East, Christian missionaries joined Muslims in attacking the Baha'i Faith. They published and circulated false and misleading information on Baha'i practices and motives. There have been incidents in Europe as well. In Germany in the mid-20th century, Protestants and Catholics protested the building of a Baha'i house of worship. As late as the 1990s, a district court in Germany denied Baha'is the right to register their local assembly as a corporation, as German law requires all religious bodies to do. The Baha'is had to sue. The German high court reversed the district court's decision, saying that it was obvious that the Baha'i Faith was indeed an independent religion.

Persecution in Iran

Perhaps nowhere in the world have Baha'is suffered systematic persecution equal to what they have suffered in Iran, the Baha'i Faith's birthplace. Baha'is are still viewed by the government as heretics and enemies of Islam. The Baha'i community is the largest religious minority in Iran, with approximately 350,000 members. Unlike Zoroastrians, who also follow a religion that began in Iran and who are a protected minority under Iranian law, Baha'is have no civil rights there.

Shortly after the Islamic Republic took control of Iran in 1979, the government began a severe crackdown on Baha'i activities. They seized Baha'i property and destroyed shrines and cemeteries. Baha'is in jobs with government oversight were fired, their pensions cancelled, and their savings seized. Baha'is were banned from attending Iranian schools and universities. Baha'i schools were banned as well. The authorities arrested prominent members of the community and charged them as spies. Many were executed.

In 1983, Iranian authorities arrested 10 Baha'i women and girls. They were accused of teaching children about the Baha'i Faith. In Iran, teaching the Baha'i Faith to Muslims is punishable by death. The authorities offered the women to renounce the Baha'i Faith and accept Islam. The women refused and were executed. In all, more than 200 Baha'is were executed or killed, and hundreds more were imprisoned for the "crime" of being members of the Baha'i Faith.

An outcry from the world community brought some relief. Canada, the European Parliament, and the United States Congress denounced Iran's actions. The United Nations, through its Human Rights Council, has pressured Iran to stop its official persecution of Baha'is. Much of the most violent persecution had stopped by the 1990s. However, as recently as 1997, a Baha'i was executed for allegedly converting a Muslim to the Baha'i Faith. Baha'is in Iran continue to experience discrimination in education, jobs, housing, travel, and practice of religion.

Challenges for the Future

The kind of growth that the Baha'i Faith has experienced in the last century brings with it new challenges. One challenge is that of maintaining a unified community. Once a religion composed almost entirely of Muslims of Iranian descent, it now encompasses cultures and peoples of all backgrounds, nationalities, and races. Its followers come from both highly literate and technologically advanced countries and from countries where few people read and write. Baha'i philosophy states that all people are equal in the sight of God, but it recognizes vast differences in opportunity. Still, it will be a challenge for the faith, with its limited membership, to encourage a skeptical world that seems torn apart by ethnic, national, and religious strife.

Another challenge is that of participation. With no professional clergy or missionaries and no funding from outside sources, the Baha'i Faith depends entirely on its members to do the work of the faith. One of the strongest features of the faith is that everyone is expected to contribute to the community. Its goal is to build a society that will eventually be global in scope. The Universal House of Justice has said that

> . . . the participation of every believer is of the utmost importance, and is a source of power and vitality. . . . If every believer will carry out these sacred duties, we shall be astonished at the accession of power which will result to the whole body, and which in turn will give rise to further growth and a showering of greater blessings on all of us.

■ **Countries with Baha'i Radio Stations**
Bolivia
Chile
Ecuador
Panama
Peru
United States

Most Baha'i communities around the world have begun with the work of pioneers. Over the last few years, these new communities have become self-governing and self-sustaining; but there is much work to be done. The young communities are charged not only with governing themselves but also with establishing schools, community centers, and economic development projects as well as continuing to spread the Baha'i message. If the faith is to succeed in its social and spiritual goals, it needs the active participation of every member.

Another major challenge is that of dealing with oppression, as problems in Iran have shown. Westerners mostly accept the notion of freedom of religion, but many countries where Baha'i has a presence have established religions and do not welcome other faiths.

Toward a New World Order

More than 100 years ago, Baha'u'llah spoke of a "new world order." Baha'is understand that a time of tremendous upheaval is here. The traditional political, social, and religious solutions seem not to be working; in fact, they seem to be pulling society apart. Baha'is believe that out of this time of turmoil will come a time when all humanity is united in love and brotherhood among all peoples. National rivalries will end. Global institutions will be formed. These will help to bring about harmony throughout the world. All war will end. There will be universal peace.

A new world order will not come into being quickly. But the world is changing. Racial and gender equality is slowly becoming a reality in some parts of the world. Nations are beginning to realize that they are dependent on one another for security and for economic strength. These are all things Baha'u'llah foresaw more than a century ago.

The New World Order of Baha'u'llah covers the entire range of human activity. It is not only a change in the political life of the world, but a revolution in its social, cultural, spiritual, and economic life as well. Baha'is believe that the New World Order is the will of God, and that God wants humanity to be united. They work toward bringing the New World Order about.

Baha'is and World Peace

Baha'is believe that peace is the result of determination and attitude. Before there can be world peace, there must be a will among all nations to have peace on Earth. This will comes from spiritual and moral resources.

War continues to be a terrible feature of modern times. All nations speak of the longing for peace, but they seem unable to

---

■ The Destiny of America and the Promise of World Peace

The American nation, Baha'is believe, will evolve through tests and trials to become a land of spiritual distinction and leadership, a champion of justice and unity among all peoples and nations, and a powerful servant of the cause of everlasting peace. This is the peace promised by God in the sacred texts of the world's religions.

Establishing peace is . . . a complex task requiring a new level of commitment to resolving issues not customarily associated with the pursuit of peace.

Universal acceptance of the spiritual principle of the oneness of humankind is essential to any successful attempt to establish world peace.

Racism, one of the most baneful and persistent evils, is a major barrier to peace.

The emancipation of women, the achievement of full equality of the sexes, is one of the most important, though less acknowledged, prerequisites of peace.

The inordinate disparity between rich and poor keeps the world in a state of instability, preventing the achievement of peace.

Unbridled nationalism, as distinguished from a sane and legitimate patriotism, must give way to a wider loyalty, to the love of humanity as a whole.

Religious strife, the cause of innumerable wars and conflicts throughout history, is a major obstacle to progress. The challenge facing the world's religious leaders is to . . . work together for the advancement of human understanding and peace.

Baha'is pray, "May this American Democracy be the first nation to establish the foundation of international agreement. May it be the first nation to proclaim the unity of mankind. May it be the first to unfurl the standard of the Most Great Peace. . . ."

—National Spiritual Assembly of the Baha'is in the United States

---

■ *One of Baha'i's best-known figures was jazz trumpeter John Birks "Dizzy" Gillespie (1917–1993). Known as the "King of Bop" in the 1940s, he played with most of the famous jazz bands of his era. Of the Baha'i Faith, he wrote in his memoirs: "Becoming a Baha'i changed my life in every way. . . . I became more spiritually aware, and when you're spiritually aware, that will be reflected in what you do."*

achieve it. Baha'is identify the barriers to world peace as nationalism, racism, poverty, and religious strife. They believe that the Baha'i Faith offers a practical model for breaking down these barriers.

The Baha'i Faith as a Model for World Society

Baha'u'llah teaches that all of humanity is one people. He wrote that the time had come to unify all the people in the world into one global society. Barriers of race, creed, class, worship, and nationalism will fall. They will give way to a single, unified civilization.

In order for this new world civilization to come into being, say Baha'is, people must follow the principles Baha'u'llah laid out. They must recognize that humankind is one and eliminate all forms of prejudice. They must bring about full equality for women. They must recognize the essential oneness of all religions. They must eliminate extremes of poverty and of wealth.

People must see that science and religion are both forces for good and reconcile the two; they must achieve a balance between technology and nature. There must be universal education. People must maintain a high standard of personal conduct, with service, generosity, kindness, and good will toward others. Finally, there should be a world federal system, governing all. To many, such goals sound impossible. Yet every day, Baha'is put them into practice.

In the 21st century, the Baha'i world continues to grow and spread. Since the 1950s, when there were about 200,000 Baha'is worldwide, adherence to the faith has increased 30-fold to more than 6 million people. In the Baha'i Faith, people of all racial, ethnic, and national backgrounds come together in cooperation to pursue the goals of their faith. In creating harmony within diversity, Baha'is believe that they stand as a model for the world.

■ Countries and Territories Where the Baha'i World Community Has a Presence

Africa

Algeria
Angola
Benin
Botswana
Burkina Faso
Burundi
Cameroon
Cape Verde Islands
Central African Republic
Chad
Cosmoros
Democratic Republic of Congo
Djibouti
Egypt
Equatorial Guinea
Eritrea
Ethiopia
Gabon
Gambia
Ghana
Guinea
Guinea Bissau
Ivory Coast
Kenya
Lesotho
Liberia
Libya
Madagascar
Malawi
Mali
Mauritania
Mauritius
Morocco
Mozambique
Namibia
Niger
Nigeria
Republic of Congo
Reunion
Rwanda
St. Helena
Sahara
São Tomé and Príncipe
Senegal
Seychelles
Sierra Leone
Somalia
Somaliland
South Africa
Spanish North Africa
Sudan
Swaziland
Tanzania
Togo
Tunisia
Uganda
Zambia
Zimbabwe

Americas

Anguila
Antigua and Barbuda
Argentina
Aruba
Bahamas
Barbados
Belize
Bermuda
Bolivia
Brazil
Canada
Cayman Islands
Chile
Colombia
Costa Rica
Cuba
Dominica
Dominican Republic
Ecuador
El Salvador
Falkland Islands
French Guiana
Greenland
Grenada
Guadeloupe
Guatemala
Guyana
Haiti
Honduras
Jamaica
Martinique
Mexico
Montserrat
Netherlands Antilles
Nicaragua
Panama
Paraguay
Peru
Puerto Rico
St. Kitts and Nevis
St. Lucia
St. Pierre and Miquelon
St. Vincent and Grenadines
Suriname
Trinidad and Tobago
Turks and Caicos Islands
United States
US Virgin Islands
Uruguay
Venezuela

Asia

Afghanistan
Azerbaijan
Bangladesh
Bhutan
Cambodia
China
India
Indonesia
Japan
Laos
Malaysia
Maldives

■ Countries and Territories Where the Baha'i World Community Has a Presence (continued)

Mongolia
Myanmar (Burma)
Nepal
Pakistan
Philippines
Singapore
South Korea
Sri Lanka
Taiwan
Tajikistan
Thailand
Timor
Turkmenistan
Uzbekistan
Vietnam

Australasia
American Samoa
Australia
Cocos and Keeling Islands
Cook Islands
Fiji
French Polynesia
Guam
Kiribati
Marshall Islands
Micronesia
Nauru
New Caledonia
New Zealand
Niue Island
Northern Mariana

Islands
Palau
Papua New Guinea
Samoa
Solomon Islands
Tokelau Islands
Tonga
Tuvalu
Vanuatu
Wallis and Futuna Islands

Europe
Albania
Andorra
Armenia
Austria
Belgium
Belarus
Bulgaria
Channel Islands
Cyprus
Czech Republic
Denmark
Estonia
Faeroe Islands
Finland
France
Georgia
Germany
Gibraltar
Great Britain
Greece

Hungary
Iceland
Ireland
Isle of Man
Italy
Lichtenstein
Luxembourg
Malta
Monaco
Netherlands
Norway
Poland
Portugal
Romania
Russia
San Marino
Slovakia
Slovenia
Spain
Sweden
Switzerland
Ukraine
Yugoslavia

Middle East
Bahrain
Brunei
Iran
Iraq
Israel
Jordan
Kuwait

Lebanon
Oman
Palestine
Qatar
Saudi Arabia
Syria
Turkey
United Arab Emirates
Yemen

—World Christian Encyclopedia, 2001

CHAPTER NOTES

page 12   Baha'u'llah, *Gleanings from the Writings of Baha'u'llah*. Trans. Shoghi Effendi. Wilmette, Ill.: Baha'i Publishing Trust, 1976, p. 85

page 13   Baha'u'llah, *Gleanings from the Writings of Baha'u'llah*, p. 249

page 14   *Baha'i Prayers: A Selection of Prayers Revealed by Baha'u'llah, the Bab, and 'Abdu'l-Baha*, new ed. Wilmette, Ill.: Baha'i Publishing Trust, 1991, p. 152

page 29   H. M. Balyuzi, *The Bab*. Oxford, U.K.: George Ronald, 1973, pp. 146–147

page 31   (top) Nabil, *The Dawn-Breakers*. Trans. Shoghi Effendi. Wilmette, Ill.: Baha'i Publishing Trust, 1996, p. 514

page 31   (bottom) Shoghi Effendi, *God Passes By,* 3d ed. Wilmette, Ill.: Baha'i Publishing Trust, 1974, p. 53

page 32   Shoghi Effendi, *God Passes By*, p. 65

page 33   Nabil, *The Dawn-Breakers*, p. 411

page 38   Baha'u'llah, "Epistle to the Son of the Wolf," in J. E. Esslemont, *Baha'u'llah and the New Era, 3rd ed*. Wilmette, Ill.: Baha'i Publishing Trust, 1979, p. 39

page 39   Shoghi Effendi, *God Passes By*, p.101

page 41   Baha'u'llah, *Kitab-i-Iqan*. Trans. Shoghi Effendi. Wilmette, Ill.: Baha'i Publishing Trust, 1950, p. 251

page 43   Baha'u'llah, *Gleanings*, p. 249

page 45   Moojan Momen, *A Short Introduction to the Baha'i Faith*. Oxford, U.K.: Oneworld Publications, 1997, p. 124

page 51   Baha'u'llah, *The Hidden Words of Baha'u'llah*. Reprinted 1985, Part I, p. 3, n. 1

page 52   (top) Baha'u'llah, *Kitab-i-Iqan*, p. 109

page 52   (middle) Excerpted from *The Baha'is*, a publication of the Baha'i International Community, 1992, p. 24

page 55   Baha'u'llah, *Kitab-i-Aqdas*. Haifa, Israel: Baha'i World Centre, p. 30

page 57   Baha'u'llah, "Tablet of Ishraqat," p. 92

page 57   Baha'u'llah, *Gleanings*, p. 299

page 58   Baha'u'llah, *The Seven Valleys and the Four Valleys*. Trans. Marzeih Gail. Wilmette, Ill.: Baha'i Publishing Trust, 1978, p. 36

page 58   'Abdu'l-Baha, *Paris Talks*. London: Baha'i Publishing Trust, 1979, pp. 72, 80, 138

page 60   (top) 'Abdu'l-Baha, *Paris Talks.*, pp. 52–53

page 60   (middle) 'Abdu'l-Baha, *The Promulgation of Universal Peace,* 2d ed. Wilmette, Ill.: The Bahai Publishing Trust, 1982, p. 133

Page 60   (bottom) 'Abdu'l-Baha, *Selections from the Writings of 'Abdu'l-Baha*. Haifa, Israel: Baha'i World Centre, 1978, p. 302, n. 227

page 67   Shoghi Effendi, *The World Order of Baha'u'llah: Selected Letters*. Wilmette, Ill.: Baha'i Publishing Trust, 1991, p. 139

page 78   Baha'u'llah, *Gleanings*, p. 65, n. 27; p. 328, n. 153

page 80   Baha'u'llah, *Gleanings*, pp. 276–278, n. 128

page 81   Baha'u'llah, *The Hidden Words*. Part I, p. 2, n. 2; Part II, pp. 23–24, n. 5

page 81   'Abdu'l-Baha, *Tablets of 'Abdu'l-Baha*, quoted in *A Pattern of Baha'i Life*. London: Baha'i Publishing Trust, 1983, p. 41

page 82   (top) Baha'u'llah, *Kitab-i-Aqdas*. "Prayers and Meditations by Baha'u'llah CLXXXI," p. 101

page 82   (middle) 'Abdu'l-Baha, quoted in William S. Hatcher and J. Douglas Martin, *The Baha'i Faith: The Emerging Global Religion*. Wilmette, Ill.: Baha'i Publishing Trust, Revised Paperback Edition, 1998, p. 187

page 82   (bottom) 'Abdu'l-Baha, *Paris Talks*. London: Baha'i Publishing Trust, 1979, p. 174

page 83   'Abdu'l-Baha, *Selections*, p. 118, n. 86

page 85   (top) 'Abdu'l-Baha, quoted in *A Pattern of Baha'i Life*, p. 24

page 85   (middle) 'Abdu'l-Baha, *Selections*, p. 145, n. 86

page 85   (bottom) *Baha'i Prayers*, pp. 35–36

page 86   'Abdu'l-Baha, *Tablets of the Divine Plan*, rev. ed. Wilmette, Ill.: Baha'i Publishing Trust, 1977, p. 49

page 86   Baha'u'llah, *Gleanings*, p. 345

page 86   'Abdu'l-Baha, *Some Answered Questions*. Wilmette, Ill.: Baha'i Publishing Trust, 1981, p. 228

page 87   *Baha'i Prayers*, pp. 45–46

page 95   Shoghi Effendi, *Principles of Baha'i Administration*, 4th ed. London: Baha'i Publishing Trust, 1976, p. 63

page 98   Baha'u'llah, *Tablets of Baha'u'llah*. Haifa, Israel: Baha'i World Centre, 1978, pp. 26–27

page 100   Shoghi Effendi, *The Advent of Divine Justice*. Wilmette, Ill.: Baha'i Publishing Trust, 1984, pp. 31–32

page 101   Shoghi Effendi, *The Advent of Divine Justice*, p. 35

page 101   Shoghi Effendi, *Principles of Baha'i Administration*, pp. 22–23

page 113   Universal House of Justice, *Messages from the Universal House of Justice*, 1963–1986, no. 14.8

GLOSSARY

'Abdu'l-Baha—The Baha'i name of Abbas Effendi, son of Baha'u'llah and leader of the Baha'i Faith, 1892–1921.

Administrative Order—Rules that govern the Baha'i Faith.

Adrianople—The former name of Edirne, the city in European Turkey to which Baha'u'llah was banished.

Akka—A prison city in Palestine (in what is now part of Israel) where Baha'u'llah was imprisoned.

Aqdas—The Kitab-i-Aqdas, the Most Holy Book.

Atheists—People who do not believe in God.

Ayyam-i-Ha—The name for the days added to the Baha'i calendar to bring the total to 365 or 366.

Azalis—Supporters of Mirza Yahya (Subh-i-Azal) against Baha'u'llah for leadership of the Baha'i Faith.

Azerbaijan—An area of northwestern Iran where the Bab was imprisoned.

Bab, the—Ali Muhammad, a religious leader in Iran who founded the Babi faith. His religious name means "gate."

Babi faith—Or Babism. The religious movement founded by the Bab.

Badasht—A town in Iran; the scene of an important Babi conference.

Baha—An Arabic word meaning "glory."

Baha'i International Community—The Baha'i organization that works with the United Nations.

Baha'i World Center—The center of the Baha'i Faith, located in Haifa, Israel.

Baha'u'llah—The Baha'i name for Mirza Husayn Ali Nuri, founder of the Baha'i Faith. It means "Glory of God."

Bahji—The last home of Baha'u'llah, and a place of Baha'i pilgrimage.

Banishment—Sending someone away from his or her home country as a punishment.

Bastinado—A beating on the soles of the feet with sticks or rods, used as punishment or torture.

Bayan, The—The name of the book of rules written by the Bab.

Book of Certitude—The book in which Baha'u'llah describes divine progression (see *Kitab-i-Iqan*).

Calligraphy—A kind of stylized handwriting.

Chihriq—The name of the prison in which the Bab was kept.

Clergy—Ministers, priests, or rabbis of a faith.

Convert—Someone who leaves one religion and joins another; to change religions.

Covenant—The Baha'i spiritual agreement and pledge taken by all Baha'is.

Covenant-Breakers—Those expelled from the faith for failing to accept the Covenant of Baha'i unity.

Divine messenger—A person sent by God to teach humanity. In the Baha'i Faith, divine messengers include all founders of the world's great religions and the Bab.

Edirne—Formerly Adrianople. The city in European Turkey to which Baha'u'llah was banished.

Exile—To force someone to live away from his or her country.

Festival of Ridvan—Twelve-day celebration of Baha'u'llah's declaration.

Fireside—The name for a Baha'i gathering in which the religion is taught.

Gleanings from the Writings of Baha'u'llah—A collection of works by Baha'u'llah, read as scripture.

Guardian of the Faith, Guardianship—Term for a leader of the Baha'i Faith; the position held by Shoghi Effendi.

Haifa—The city in Israel where the Baha'i World Center is located.

Hands of the Cause of God—Group of leaders appointed to assist in Baha'i administration.

Heresy—A religious belief that goes against established church doctrines.

Heretic—Someone denounced by the church for holding beliefs contrary to established faith.

Hidden Imam—In Shi'ah Islam, the twelfth religious leader in a line established by the Prophet Muhammad. The Hidden Imam is expected to come again to lead the Muslim people.

Hidden Words, The—A book of instruction written by Baha'u'llah (see *Kalimat-i-Maknunih*).

Huququ'llah—"Right of God"; the voluntary wealth tax paid by Baha'is to support the faith.

Imam—Term used by Muslims for a religious leader.

Infidel—An unbeliever; someone who does not believe in the predominating religion.

Intercession—Prayer offered on behalf of another.

Iqan—The Kitab-i-Iqan, the Book of Certitude.

Islam—The religion begun by the Prophet Muhammad and widely practiced in the Middle East.

Jihad—Holy war.

Kalimat-i-Maknunih—The Hidden Words, a book written by Baha'u'llah.

Kitab-i-Aqdas—Most Holy Book, a book of rules for the Baha'i Faith written by Baha'u'llah.

Kitab-i-Iqan—Book of Certitude, a book written by Baha'u'llah.

Koran—The holy book of Islam.

Letters of the Living—The name for the first eighteen converts to the Babi faith, so named by the Bab.

Madhi—Arabic name for the Hidden Imam.

Maku—Fortress in Azerbaijan where the Bab was imprisoned.

Martyrdom—Death or suffering because of one's beliefs.

Mashriqu'l-Adhkar—A Baha'i house of worship.

Mirza Yahya—Half brother of Baha'u'llah who plotted against him (see *Subh-i-Azal*).

Monogamy—The practice of having only one wife.

Mosque—Muslim house of worship.

Most Holy Book—The Aqdas, or Baha'i book of divine rules (see *Kitab-i-Aqdas*).

Muhammad—The name of the prophet who proclaimed Islam.

Muhammad, Siyyid—Supporter of Mirza Yahya against Baha'u'llah.

Mulla Husayn—An early follower of the Bab; one of the Letters of the Living.

Mullah—The name for a Muslim clergyman.

New World Order—A coming time of universal peace and unity under Baha'i principles.

Nineteen-Day Feast—The first day of each Baha'i month when Baha'is gather as a community to read scripture, discuss issues, and share refreshments.

Obligatory—Required, as a prayer or a fast.

Ottoman Empire—The empire of the Turks, c. 1300–1918, encompassing parts of Europe, Asia, and Africa.

Penal colony—A place in which people who have committed crimes are confined.

Persia—The former name of Iran.

Pioneers, pioneering—The Baha'i tradition of moving to other localities or countries to establish the Baha'i Faith there.

Progressive Revelation—The unfolding of God's plan for humanity through the teachings of different religious leaders over the ages.

Quddus—A follower of the Bab; one of the Letters of the Living.

Ridvan Declaration—Baha'u'llah's sharing with his followers the revelation that he is a divine messenger.

Ridvan—An Arabic word meaning "paradise"; the garden on an island in the Tigris River where Baha'u'llah addressed his followers.

Shah—The name for the ruler of Persia (Iran).

Shaykh Tabarsi—A shrine used as a fortress by Babis when they were attacked.

Shi'ah—A Muslim sect, dominant in Persia/Iran.

Shoghi Effendi—The grandson of 'Abdu'l-Baha; Guardian of the Baha'i Faith, 1921–1957.

Siyah-Chal—The Black Pit, a prison where Baha'u'llah was held.

Siyyid—The title of respect used by Muslims who trace their ancestry back to the Prophet Muhammad.

Spiritual assembly—The name for an organized group of Baha'is.

Subh-i-Azal—Mirza Yahya, half brother of Baha'u'llah.

Sufis—Islamic mystics.

Tablet of Ishraqat—Part of the Aqdas; letter of instruction from Baha'u'llah to the Baha'i faithful.

Tahirih—A woman poet and follower of the Bab; one of the Letters of the Living.

Twelfth Imam—In Twelver Shi'ah, the One Who Would Arise; the Hidden Imam or Madhi.

Twelver Shi'ah—A form of Islam with the belief that the Twelfth Imam will return.

Universal House of Justice—The highest governing body in the Baha'i Faith.

Vahid—An early follower of Babism.

Ya Baha'u'l-Abha—Arabic for "O Glory of the All-Glorious," the Baha'i invocation.

FOR FURTHER READING

Baha'is, The. New York: Office of Public Information, Baha'i International Community, 2002.

Baha'u'llah. *The Hidden Words of Baha'u'llah*. Translated by Shoghi Effendi. Wilmette, Ill.: Baha'i Publishing Trust, 1932, 1985.

Baha'u'llah: The Central Figures, Vol. I. New York: Baha'i International Community, Office of Public Information, 2001.

Faizi, Gloria. *The Baha'i Faith: An Introduction*. Wilmette, Ill.: Baha'i Publishing Trust, 1986.

Meyer, Zoe. *Children's Stories from the Dawn-Breakers*. Wilmette, Ill.: Baha'i Publishing Trust, 1955, 2000.

Momen, Moojan. *A Short Introduction to the Baha'i Faith*. Oxford, U.K.: Oneworld Publications, 1997.

O God, Guide Me: A Selection of Prayers from Baha'u'llah, the Bab, and 'Abdu'l-Baha. Wilmette, Ill.: The Baha'i Publishing Trust, 1986, 2000.

Ronald, George. *Vignettes from the Life of 'Abdu'l-Baha, Revised Edition*. Oxford, U.K.: Oneworld Publications, 1991. Reprinted 1997.

Smith, Peter. *A Short History of the Baha'i Faith*. Oxford, U.K.: Oneworld Publications, 1995.

Treasury of Baha'i Prayers, A: Selections from the Writings of Baha'u'llah, the Bab, and 'Abdu'l-Baha. Oxford, U.K.: Oneworld Publications, 1999.

Vickers, Patrick. *The Baha'i Faith*. Oxford, U.K.: Oneworld Publications, 1992.

INDEX

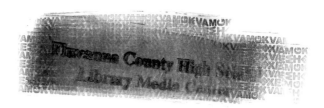
	DATE DUE		
17 NOV 2003			